Living with a
German
Shepherd Dog

Edited by
Angela Ibbotson

RINGPRESS

The Question of Gender
**_The 'he' pronoun is used throughout this book in favour of
the rather impersonal 'it', but no gender bias is intended at all._**

Published by Ringpress Books Ltd,
a division of Interpet Publishing,
Vincent Lane, Dorking, Surrey, RH4 3YX, UK
Tel: 01306 873822 Fax: 01306 885009

Series Director: Claire Horton-Bussey

Designed by Rob Benson.

First Published 2000
© 2000 RINGPRESS BOOKS

ISBN 13 : 978 1 86054 108 7
ISBN 10 : 1 86054 108 9

Printed and bound in China through Printworks International Limited

0 9 8 7 6 5 4 3 2

CONTENTS

CHAPTER ONE

INTRODUCING THE GERMAN SHEPHERD DOG

The history of the German Shepherd Dog dates back just over 100 years, which makes it a relative newcomer in the canine world. However, its shepherding ancestors date back to some of the earliest dogs in history – those versatile animals who would watch over and guard sheep and cattle.

From earliest times, dogs were bred for their working skills – it did not matter what an individual looked like, as long as he could cope with the demands of the job. If a dog proved particularly successful in a locality, he would be bred from, whatever his size or shape. So, 19th-century Germany saw a number of very different-looking shepherd dogs varying in size, colour, ear-carriage and build. Dogs from southern Germany, working in mountainous areas, developed powerful hindquarters so they could herd the sheep on the steep slopes, whereas those in more central parts of the country needed the stamina to be able to trot

The first German Shepherds were used to herd and guard sheep – and the breed still retains this working instinct.

effortlessly for mile after mile across fairly flat terrain.

It was only towards the very end of the 1800s that efforts were made to create and maintain a 'German Shepherd Dog' – an easily recognisable breed, based on the most successful working specimens.

Dog shows were becoming increasingly popular during this time, and fanciers were keen to exhibit their breeds. One fancier, Max Riechelmann, had some success with his 'German Sheepdog' called Phylax von Eulau. However, when Phylax competed against working dogs, there were very noticeable differences. This led to fears that the new breed would be contaminated almost before it was properly established, and the true working ability would be lost.

Father Of The Breed

The so-called 'Father of the Breed', Max Emil Frederick von Stephanitz, a cavalry officer, came to the rescue, and it was through his endeavours that the German Shepherd Dog was developed on pure working lines. In 1899, Captain Max von Stephanitz set up the *Verein für Deutsche Schäferhunde,* a breed club whose aims included the protection of the working German Shepherd as a breed. Within a short period of time, a distinct type had developed. This was the result of von Stephanitz's strict control over the breeding of dogs. The club, with von Stephanitz as its president, passed a series of regulations regarding the development of the breed which included:

- The minimum age at which a bitch could be bred from.
- A maximum age for stud dogs.
- Dogs that should not be bred from.
- Sires and dams who should be mated together.
- The number of puppies that should be raised from each litter.

In 1899, the same year in which the *Verein* was founded, von Stephanitz bought Horand von Graforth, a tall, powerful animal, who became the first registered dog with the Club, and the first 'official' German Shepherd in the world.

Horand Von Graforth

Stephanitz saw Horand as the ideal German Shepherd, writing:

"... he was large... with powerful bones, beautiful lines and a nobly-formed head; clean and sinewy in build, the whole dog was one livewire."

As well as Horand's physical traits, von Stephanitz also detailed his character – and what a character!

"His character corresponded to his exterior qualities: marvellous in his obedient faithfulness to his master; and above all, the straightforward nature of a gentleman with a boundless and irrepressible zest for living. Although untrained in his puppyhood, nevertheless obedient to the slightest nod when at his master's side; but when left to himself the maddest rascal, the wildest ruffian and an incorrigible promoter of strife. Never idle, always on the go; well-disposed to

The police dog par excellence, the German Shepherd has been adopted by security forces throughout the world.

harmless people but no cringer, crazy about children, with a full capacity for loving."

The first Breed Standard, written by von Stephanitz, was based on Horand. It is very detailed, as you would expect of a man who was pursuing his own vision of the ideal Shepherd. The Standard includes measurements and angle degrees, leaving little to personal interpretation – or misinterpretation.

Von Stephanitz also judged at the breed's annual dog show, the *Sieger*, where the best dog and bitch (*Sieger* and *Siegerin*) were selected. This ensured that the type outlined by von Stephanitz in the Standard was firmly established over a number of years.

Rise And Fall

As president of the *Verein*, now the largest breed club in the world, von Stephanitz had not only created a particular type of dog, but also worked to make it the popular breed that it is today. He was quick to see the potential of the breed for police work. Although his early approaches to the police were laughed off, he persevered and eventually the dogs were tried. The rest, as they say, is history; today, the German Shepherd is used extensively in many areas of police work across the world.

The outbreak of the First World War dealt a severe blow to the breed in Britain and America, where a few dogs had been imported. Hostile feelings towards all things German meant it was very unfashionable and unpatriotic not only to listen to Wagner and to eat sauerkraut, but also to own a German breed of dog. The American Kennel Club changed the name of the German

Sheepdog to the Shepherd Dog, and the Dachshund was rechristened the Badger Dog. No one was fooled by a simple name change, though, and anti-German sentiment was so strong that the breed declined in popularity – even in the UK, where the breed was called the Alsatian Wolfdog.

However, when soldiers returned home after the war, they told stories of the wonderful dogs they had seen that had shown so much courage and intelligence.

Rin Tin Tin

Lee Duncan, was one such soldier. The American came back with more than just tales of the fantastic German dogs he saw – he actually brought one back!

After training Rinty, Lee launched the dog's film career, as one of the most famous dogs in film history – Rin Tin Tin. The dog's adventures were incredibly popular and earned him many fans, and, as a result, every home wanted their own heroic Rin Tin Tin.

The breed's profile and popularity grew. Sadly, unscrupulous breeders seized the opportunity to exploit the growing demand for Shepherd puppies, and flooded the market with dogs of questionable temperament. By the end of the 1920s, the breed had a reputation for being aggressive and unpredictable. Fortunately, a committed band of breed enthusiasts, on both sides of the Atlantic, continued to strive for the ideal Shepherd, importing quality dogs to redress the balance.

In 1931, the American Kennel Club restored 'German' to the breed name after the anti-German feeling from the First World War had abated; so it was in the US that the breed

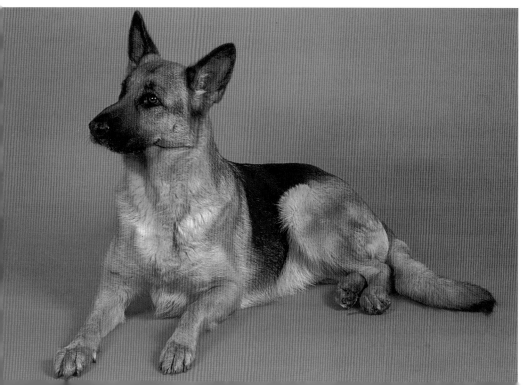

Breeders have worked hard to preserve the breed's superb temperament.

A distinguished show dog, the German Shepherd is equally highly-prized as a wonderful companion.

became known as the German Shepherd Dog for the first time.

In 1924, the UK Kennel Club dropped the 'Wolfdog', a name that had done nothing to endear the breed to the public, but it was not until 1936, the same year that von Stephanitz died, that the breed's German origins were recognised and the breed became the Alsatian (German Shepherd Dog). In 1974, it became the German Shepherd Dog (Alsatian).

Second World War

Although anti-German feeling was high during the Second World War, it was mainly directed towards Hitler and his government, and German Shepherds did not suffer more than any of the other breeds that were struggling to survive against a background of food shortages.

After the Second World War the breed experienced various dips and peaks in popularity, but it has now become firmly established as one of the most popular breeds in the world. The German Shepherd Dog consistently reaches the top positions in the annual American Kennel Club and the Kennel Club registration figures, rubbing shoulders with the ever-popular Labrador Retriever and Golden Retriever.

The Breed Today

For a relatively new breed, the German Shepherd has quickly captured the hearts of dog lovers around the world. His love of people, his eagerness to please and to share his life with his family, together with his keen intelligence, have ensured his status as companion dog *par excellence*.

From his humble beginnings as a shepherd in Germany, the German Shepherd Dog now works for police, army, fire, and search-and-rescue organisations, and is a hard-working assistance (service) dog for those that are physically disadvantaged.

The German Shepherd is the dog born to serve.

CHAPTER TWO

PUPPY POWER

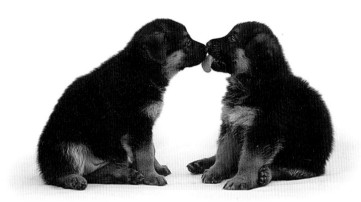

Raising a puppy can be exhausting work – always second-guessing the pup's next move, and having endless patience and endurance in training him. But the rewards are great. German Shepherds are very responsive, sensitive dogs, and the puppy months are crucial for establishing the early ground rules and cementing the foundations of your relationship.

FINDING THE RIGHT PUP

Be Prepared

When you first get a pup, it is easy to wish that he will always remain as cute, and never have to grow up; after a few months, however, you may find yourself praying for the relative calm of your dog's adulthood!

Before falling for that fluffy, floppy-eared German Shepherd puppy, you should make sure you are absolutely committed to dog ownership.

- Do you have a lifestyle that means the dog will not be left for any length of time?
- Can you fulfil the exercise demand?
- Do you have the time to devote to on-going socialisation and training?
- Can you afford the food and veterinary bills?
- Do you have time to groom the dog regularly?
- Finally, are you sure you will remain as committed for the next 14 years or so, and that your circumstances will still accommodate responsible dog ownership?

If you have answered 'no' to any of these questions, you should reconsider having a dog – especially one as demanding as a German Shepherd.

Finding A Breeder

A breeder is not only responsible for planning the litter, he/she is also responsible for introducing the puppies to the world. If the

It is important to see the puppies' close relatives – particularly the mother, as her temperament and appearance will give you some idea of how the puppies will turn out.

pups are given lots of love, attention and early socialisation, they will grow up thinking the world is a nice place to be. If they are stuck in a shed in the backyard, with little contact with anyone or anything other than their dam and littermates, you will really have your work cut out.

The busier the breeder's household, the better. Pups who are used to everyday household noises – the vacuum cleaner, washing machine etc. – should settle well into their new home with their family.

Do not be offended if the breeder interrogates you. A responsible breeder will want to be absolutely certain that their precious pups will be well cared for in their new homes and have the best homes possible. Home-checks and references are not unusual.

The breeder should also offer after-sales advice. Someone that cares for their litter will want you to call if you have problems or queries – not just for the first few weeks, but for the entirety of the dog's life.

Make sure you see the puppies' mother, and other close relatives if possible. This will give you an indication of how the puppies will turn out, both physically and mentally. The mother should have a sound, friendly temperament and should look healthy (bearing in mind she is a new mum). You should research the pedigree lines for any recurrent hereditary breed problems, and should check that the pups are clean, healthy and full of life.

If you are at all dissatisfied with the breeder, the dam or the pups, find another breeder.

Choosing Your Pup

Most prospective purchasers have firm ideas as to whether they want a dog or a bitch. Generally, there is very little difference between the two, although the male is bigger and more powerfully built. Many people say a bitch is more faithful, but dog owners dispute this. Really, it is a matter of whether you prefer the feminine or the masculine look, and whether you can cope with the inconvenience of a

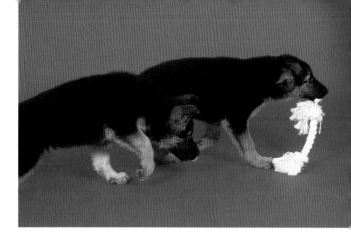

bitch's season. Obviously, neutering is an option for either dog or bitch if you have no plans to breed (see Chapter Three).

Once you have decided on the sex, it is time to choose the actual German Shepherd you will be taking home. Many breeders will have already ear-marked a pup or two for themselves to keep. It is best to be guided by the breeder as to which puppy you choose. After living with the litter for some time, the breeder will be in a better position to advise you as to which personality is best for you. For example, a very forward, dominant pup may seem cute and precocious at eight weeks, but may prove too much of a handful for an inexperienced owner as it matures. Similarly, a doe-eyed, timid little bundle in the corner is hard to resist, but may need as much knowledgeable handling by an experienced Shepherd owner, as the very confident pup.

If you are interested in showing your pup, you should ask your breeder for advice on a pup with show potential.

The Waiting Game

Most puppies are ready to go to their new homes at eight weeks of age. Before the big day arrives, there are certain preparations to make. The first step is to puppy-proof your house and garden. Shepherds are athletic, working dogs, and will make easy work of a short or rickety fence. Your garden should be fully fenced to at least six feet, and the fence foundations should be deep. As well as being good jumpers and climbers, German Shepherds are also

Watch the puppies playing together, and you will see their personalities start to emerge.

accomplished diggers!

Your home must be made safe for the puppy – he should not be able to get access to any dangerous household substances, such as cleaning materials. Either put them in top cupboards or shelves, or invest in cupboard safety-locks. Anything that you would not like to see chewed should be put away, not only for your own convenience, but also for the pup's health. Every day, vets remove the most bizarre items from pups' stomachs – objects that could prove fatal if the blockage is not dealt with urgently.

At last it is time to collect your puppy.

Journey Home

At last, the time has come to collect your puppy. With all the excitement, the journey home may be nerve-wracking for you both. To minimise the stress of the unfamiliar circumstances, leave a blanket with the breeder a couple of weeks before bringing the pup home, and ask for it to be put in the litter's bedding. The pup will then get accustomed to your smell in a warm, safe environment, and when it comes to taking him home, he will have the security of his blanket – which will not only have traces of your scent, but will also have all the familiar smells from his breeder's home.

It is advisable to take a driver with you so that you can give all your attention to your puppy on the journey, cradling and reassuring him. The breeder is unlikely to feed the pup prior to departure, but if your pup is ill, do not be too concerned, as it is only natural on what is likely to be his first long journey. Equip yourself with kitchen paper and a towel for such eventualities or for any other accidents that may happen. Water should also be available, particularly if the journey is lengthy, and if it is a warm day (in which case, good ventilation in the vehicle is also essential).

Family Introductions

German Shepherds are inquisitive creatures, and puppies are especially so. Your pup will be fascinated with all the new smells and people in your home, and will want to investigate. Let him explore the garden, meet the family, and investigate the kitchen and living room – and that will be enough for one day. It is very important not to overwhelm the new arrival, so try to maintain a calm atmosphere, particularly if you have children who are bound to be over-excited.

First Night

Like babies, puppies need a lot of sleep. After the introductions are over, give him his first meal, take him out to the garden to relieve himself, and settle him in his bed. Cosy bedding in a puppy crate, situated in a quiet corner of the house (e.g. in the kitchen), makes a safe and comfortable den.

If your Shepherd is unsettled on his first night, do not be too concerned. It will be the first time he has slept away from his dam and littermates, and he will still be unused to his new surroundings.

Some owners recommend ignoring the pup, believing that getting up in the night to see to him will teach him that barking and crying is a sure way of getting your attention, thereby setting a precedent for many sleepless nights to come. Others recommend attending to him, so that he is reassured in his new environment. Taking him into your bed can be unwise – unless you intend to have a fully-grown adult Shepherd sharing your bed for the next 12 years or so. Your puppy will have to get used to sleeping alone at some point – and it may as well be from the very start.

Feeding

You are what you eat, or rather, your dog is what

Periods of activity are interspersed with long periods of rest.

you feed him, so diet is a very important aspect of your pup's care, especially with a large breed such as the German Shepherd. Your breeder should provide you with a diet sheet to follow, and it is important that you adhere to it for at least the first few days of getting your pup home.

If you want to change his diet, and use a new brand of food, it should be done very gradually. This will allow the pup to get used to his new food, without it being a shock to his system and resulting in tummy upsets. Put just a spoonful of the new food into his meal, and a spoonful less of his former food. Gradually increase over the course of several days, correspondingly putting in less of the former food, until a complete change-over has been achieved.

When you first get your German Shepherd puppy, he is likely to be on four meals a day. This is generally cut to three meals when the pup is around 12 weeks. If your puppy leaves one of his feeds, or doesn't eat all of it, use the same daily food ration but divide it into three

meals. The same can be done when he goes down to two meals – one in the morning and one in the evening. This is generally done at around six months of age. Some owners cut down to just one meal eventually, feeding his entire daily ration in one go; others prefer to continue with two feeds.

Remember that your German Shepherd should always have access to fresh water.

FAMILY LIFE

German Shepherds love people – and will take well to family life, as long as they are treated with respect. Although they often have a 'favourite', they bond closely with all their 'pack'. Interestingly, their favourite family member is not necessarily the person who feeds them (German Shepherds are not so easily bribed!), but, rather, the person who trains them and who gains their respect that way.

With their naturally protective instincts, some German Shepherds can focus on their 'favourite' and may become unresponsive to other family members. It is therefore important to show your pup from a very early age, that he should respond to everyone in the house – even children. Including all family members in the training of the pup will help to gain the pup's respect and should lay the foundations for a happy home life.

Children
Children and German Shepherds usually enjoy each other's company, and will develop a close

It is wise to feed your puppy the diet he is used to in order to avoid stomach upsets.

relationship. However, children and dogs – of any breed – should always be supervised. This is as much for the dog's safety as for the children's.

Some breeders may be reluctant to home a German Shepherd pup with a family with young children; again, this is often for the dog's sake. Generally, having children is good preparation – rearing puppies and children is not so very different! If prospective owners arrive to view the litter and the accompanying children are very badly behaved, it is generally a sign that the parents lack the discipline needed to raise a German Shepherd properly.

Children should learn the following rules:

- Play should be controlled. Repeated short bursts of high-energy activities are not good for the pup. A German Shepherd never knows when to stop. If there is fun to be had, he wants a slice of the action, and can easily overexert himself.

- Never disturb the pup when he is sleeping, or eating, or is in his bed. His sleeping area should be guaranteed to offer undisturbed 'time-out', and should be a strictly child-free zone.

- Never take the pup's bowl or toys away when he is eating or playing. The exercises on page 21 are designed to prevent the dog becoming over-possessive, but children should also be taught to respect the dog and to leave him in peace.

Puppies and children must learn mutual respect.

- Never tease the pup. Apart from it being unkind and unnecessary, German Shepherds have long memories, and may bear the grudge well into adulthood.

Teaching Respect

With proper training and socialisation, the German Shepherd can be one of the best family dogs in the world. However, because they are so intelligent – sometimes outsmarting their owners – they can be difficult to control if they do not respect their family.

German Shepherds are a naturally dominant breed, and your pup should be shown that he is subordinate to everyone in the family – regardless of age. A German Shepherd likes to know the ground rules, and will be happier knowing he is bottom of the family pack than being confused by signals over his status.

The most important consideration when training a German Shepherd is to remember that he likes order and discipline. Discipline should not be cruel or punitive – German Shepherds are far too sensitive for that, and much harm can be done. The best method is to instil kind and effective discipline where bad behaviour is ignored, and good behaviour is rewarded. Rewards can be praise, petting, a game or a tasty treat. Remember always to be consistent in whatever rules you set, so that the dog does not get confused.

The following exercises will provide the foundation of good manners in your German Shepherd – which is essential when living with such a large breed. Everyone in the family should do these exercises with the pup (remembering to supervise children when they are training).

Bite Inhibition

Teaching a dog not to bite is very important in all breeds, but is especially significant with a breed as large as the German Shepherd. If your pup is not taught that biting hurts, he will grow up thinking that it is acceptable. As he gets larger, he will not realise his own strength and may cause injury without intending to.

With a breed as naturally protective as the German Shepherd, the last thing you should ever encourage is aggression of any kind. Instead, you should show your pup that teeth must *never* be used on people. If the pup mouths (as all puppies do), make a high-pitched yelp, turn away from him and ignore him. This will show him that it hurts and is unacceptable behaviour.

Be consistent. If, when playing, he gets over-excited and chews you instead of a toy, yelp and ignore – even if you know he did it by accident. It will teach him to play more gently, and to be especially careful in future.

Gently

As a continuation of the bite inhibition exercise, the pup needs to learn to be gentle when dealing with people.

- Hold a treat in your hand and offer it to the pup, telling him to take it "Gently".
- If he attempts to snap, do not let him have

Practise giving treats by hand, and this will teach your puppy not to grab and use his teeth.

the treat. Say "No" and hold the treat firmly in your hand so he cannot take it.

- If he snaps, it is important not to pull your hand away, as this is only likely to encourage him to snap next time (to get it before he anticipates it will be taken away).
- If, when attempting to take the treat, he nips your finger, yelp and ignore him (as for Bite Inhibition, above).
- Whenever he takes the treat gently – no snapping or biting – he should be praised handsomely.
- Only when the pup is consistently taking treats gently from adults should the exercises be done with children (under supervision, of course).

Treats In Bowl

German Shepherds were bred to guard, and it doesn't take much to unleash this instinct in them. Food and toys can be a particularly sensitive area if early steps are not taken to prevent a problem arising. A few minutes' training each day is a worthwhile investment, as possessive guarding can be a difficult problem to overcome once established.

- When your pup is eating a meal, pop an even tastier treat in his bowl, so that he learns to welcome hands reaching for his bowl.
- After a few sessions, pick his food bowl up to put the treat in. This way, he learns to look forward to his bowl being taken away, knowing that something mouthwatering will be put in it.

A hand putting an extra treat into the food bowl will be welcomed, and not seen as a threat.

- Repeat the exercise with everyone in the family, so that your pup will accept his bowl being taken away with not so much as a grumble.
- It is useful to repeat this exercise occasionally as top-up training throughout the dog's life.

Sharing Toys

The German Shepherd can also become possessive of his toys. If properly socialised, most German Shepherds do not develop problems, but it is better to be safe than sorry, and to safeguard against them just in case.

- When your German Shepherd is still a young pup, give him a toy and play with him.
- When he has it in his mouth, hold the toy and pull very gently, while telling him to "Give". Do not pull too hard, as you may damage his teeth. The aim is not to pull it

The Shepherd puppy must learn to share his toys, and give them up when requested.

out of his mouth, but for him to release his hold on the toy.

- When he lets go, make a huge fuss of him, give him a treat, and give him the toy straight back. He will learn that, although his toy is a good possession, letting someone else have it is just as rewarding.
- Once your Shepherd pup knows the "Give" command, let other family members, including children, practise it.

Raising Cats And Dogs

German Shepherds and cats generally get on well together. Although problems are rare, you should not assume they are going to get along famously, and should introduce the two very carefully. German Shepherds are big dogs and could seriously hurt a cat if they are not taught

to treat them gently and with respect. Similarly, a cat can damage a pup's eyes with her claws if she feels intimidated and trapped.

Cats can jump higher than dogs and will feel safe in a high position, such as on a tall cupboard, so make sure the cat has an upward escape route. This is better than leaving a door open for her to bolt, as it may encourage the pup's chase instinct and will make matters worse.

- Put the pup in his crate (see page 26) and let the cat investigate him. Reassure her all the time, stroking her, and talking in a quiet, low voice.
- Take the pup out of the crate, and hold and cuddle him.
- Ask a friend or family member to hold and cuddle the cat.
- Do not force the cat to stay if she doesn't want to. If she wishes to escape, let her. Keep hold of the pup, though, so that he cannot chase or jump on her.
- Encourage the pup to look away from the cat. Every time he looks at you instead of the cat, give him a treat. Withhold the treat when he won't take his eyes off the cat.
- When the intense fascination with the cat has worn off, and you are able to get him to look at you instead of at her all the time, you can consider letting them get to know each other a little more.
- Make sure the pup is on a lead, so that you can control him if he gets overexcited, and let him sniff the cat. Remain calm and

If introductions are carefully supervised, a German Shepherd and a cat can become the best of friends. Photo courtesy: Kari Selinger.

relaxed, talking, petting and praising both of them the whole time.

- Generally, the cat will reprimand the pup if he oversteps the mark. Seeing a puffed-up ball of fur hissing and spitting at him is usually enough to teach the pup to respect his feline housemate.

Resident Dogs

Some owners think it will be easier to raise a pup when an adult dog is already resident, believing that the dog can help to teach the pup some manners. This is sometimes the case, but it can also be counterproductive, with the older dog being led astray by the pup. Suddenly, instead of having two well-behaved dogs, you have two delinquents! Think seriously about whether you have the time to cope with the worst-case scenario – training a pup and retraining an adult.

Provided your existing dog has been well socialised, there should be no problems introducing the pup to him. The situation should still be handled sensitively, however, as

noses can be put out of joint. This is quite understandable: your adult will notice that, suddenly, visitors ignore your older dog and head straight for the cute little pup. Because you are likely to be spending considerable time training and socialising the pup, it is important to make sure your older dog doesn't feel left out. Put time aside where, in a puppy-free zone, you can spend time with your dog and make him feel special, too.

Introductions between adult dogs should take place in neutral territory, so that the resident dog doesn't feel defensive about the would-be 'intruder'. However, because your Shepherd pup won't have completed his puppy vaccinations, the first meeting will have to take place in your garden. Let them sniff and play with each other, but do not introduce any toys, as they can be a source of conflict.

Being pack animals, social order is very important to dogs. If your older dog growls at the pup, do not interfere (only do so if you fear a physical attack). Reprimanding the dog and then fussing over the pup will be interpreted by

Make sure you give the resident dog plenty of attention so that he does not become jealous of the new arrival.

the dogs as you elevating the pup's position over your adult dog. They will soon sort out who is top dog. Usually the adult dog assumes this role, but sometimes a very submissive adult dog is more than happy to take second place. Reinforce whatever hierarchy they eventually agree, feeding the top dog first etc.

Providing the older dog with time away from the pup is very important. German Shepherd pups are very energetic and will test the patience of even the most tolerant adult dogs. Putting the pup in a crate for his rest periods will give the adult dog some time alone to recuperate; but it is also important that, when your adult gets into his bed, he is allowed to sleep undisturbed – otherwise, tempers may fray.

EARLY LESSONS

Puppy Playgroup
As soon as your pup has protection from his vaccinations, it is vital that he learns how to behave with other dogs; puppy parties or playgroups, usually held at vet surgeries, are great for this.

• Your German Shepherd pup can meet lots of other pups and hone his doggie social skills.
• Your pup will learn that vet surgeries are fun places to be in and are not to be feared.
• You will have the opportunity of meeting other pup owners to share your experiences.

Like children, pups learn very important lessons through play. A course of play sessions in a controlled, supervised situation with a wide variety of pups is the best way of ensuring your German Shepherd doesn't become the despised park bully, destined always to play alone.

German Shepherds are big dogs. In the eyes of other dog owners, or of smaller dogs, they can be intimidating. We have all seen owners grab their small dogs and carry them off the

Your puppy needs to learn and understand the canine code of behaviour in order to become a civilised adult.
Photo courtesy: Valerie Egger.

moment a larger dog appears in the park. It may seem unfair that someone is misjudging your big softie, but other dog owners have no way of telling a good-tempered dog from a bad, and cannot risk their pets' safety. Even in well-intentioned play, a small dog can be harmed if the play becomes too boisterous.

Your pup has to learn how to interact and play with dogs of all shapes and sizes. Puppy socialisation and early obedience classes are ideal for this. There, he will learn to read doggie body language and to respond to it accordingly. This is crucial learning for when he is an adult in a park, when he will need to:

- Recognise when a dog is not interested in playing
- Appease aggressive dogs
- Show he wants to be a friend.

If he is playing too roughly, other pups will soon tell him to stop or to be more gentle, by squealing and ignoring him. Because the game then ends, your German Shepherd will learn that play must be gentle or the fun stops.

The worst thing you can do is to create problems by anticipating problems. Holding the lead tight when encountering a small dog in the park, or frantically calling your German Shepherd back in a hysterical way, will make him think that the small dog is a threat. German Shepherds are very sensitive to their owners' moods, and will react to them quickly, so always act in a relaxed way.

House-training

German Shepherds are very intelligent dogs and will quickly learn to be clean in the house. Choose a spot in the garden where you would like your pup to eliminate, and take him there every two hours (sooner if he still has accidents), plus:

- Last thing at night and first thing in the morning
- Immediately after eating
- Before and after exercise
- After periods of excitement – playing with visitors etc.
- Whenever you see him sniffing the ground and circling.

When he is on his spot in the garden, tell him to "Get busy", or any other phrase you would prefer (remember that you will have to say it in public). When he eliminates, praise him madly, and then spend some time together playing before returning to the house. Do not go straight back in or the pup will realise that he gets to be outside longer by crossing his legs.

Accidents Happen

If you catch him in the act, clap your hands to get his attention and to stop him in mid-flow, and encourage him outside in a fun, excited way. Never shout at the pup or punish him for having an accident – he is just answering a call of nature. If you take him out regularly, and are attentive to him, no accidents should take place.

If an accident does happen, clean it up thoroughly with a special cleaner designed for the job. Ordinary disinfectants may remove the smell to a human nose, but a sensitive German Shepherd nose will still be able to smell the odour, and your pup will be encouraged to eliminate there again.

Chewing

If you have never had a puppy before, you will be surprised at how much damage can be done by something so small and angelic-looking. A puppy's needle-sharp teeth and craving to chew means he can demolish shoes, bags, furniture... anything in his path.

Keep anything you do not want destroyed out of his reach – not only to save you a fortune in replacing endless pairs of slippers etc., but also to protect the puppy's life. Swallowing something that is poisonous, or that gets lodged in his throat or stomach, could be very dangerous for your pup.

Provide your pup with suitable toys to satisfy his craving to chew. Buy good-quality, durable toys and check regularly for damage. Tough rubber toys are often popular with pups. Replace any toys that could pose a threat to your pup – particularly toys where the plastic squeak could be swallowed.

Crates

Puppies can get into all sorts of mischief in a very short time. For your German Shepherd's safety – and your sanity – it is useful to have somewhere secure to put the pup while you are unable to give him your undivided attention, while getting the shopping in from the car, while you have visitors who aren't too keen on dogs, etc. Crates are incredibly handy – not just for puppyhood but for all the dog's life. As long as it is a comfortable den, and is not used as a

Provide safe, durable toys for your puppy to chew when he is teething.

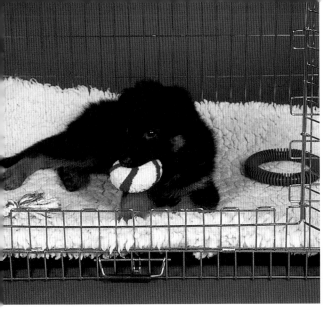

Make the crate attractive to your puppy, with soft bedding, and toys to play with.

punishment, your pup will learn to love his crate as much as you do.

Make it as appealing as possible – with some cosy bedding, a couple of safe toys, and perhaps a blanket over the top to keep out draughts and to make it more private and enclosed.

Cars

Crates are also a godsend for when you wish to introduce the pup to car travel. Getting the pup to enjoy being in the car is worth every effort – having a whining, barking, vomiting pup is bad enough, but when it is a fully-grown adult, it really is no fun at all.

The aim is to get the pup to enjoy being in the car. Many pups are wary of cars because they are not used to them and because they soon work out that all journeys seem to end at the vet's surgery. Show him that this really isn't the case.

- Pop the crate in the car, and sit the pup in it. Give him a couple of really tasty treats. Settle

him on his bedding and speak to him in a soothing, calm voice. Shut the crate door for a couple of minutes, but keep talking to him.
- Ignore him if he barks, and praise him and give treats when he is quiet.
- When he is used to sitting calmly, get someone to start the engine and keep it running for just a short time. Distract your pup with praise and a treat or two.
- Gradually extend the length of time the engine is kept on.
- When he is content with the engine running, ask the driver to drive a short distance. The journey should be as relaxed as possible – so avoid speed humps and frantic traffic hot spots. Keep reassuring the pup the whole time.
- As soon as you get home, take the pup out and have a quick game in the garden.
- Gradually extend the length of journey time.

For the driving sessions, make sure the pup hasn't recently been fed. Although it isn't the end of the world if he is car-sick, you should avoid it if at all possible. Being sick will be unpleasant for the pup, and you will then have to work to overcome his unfavourable first impressions of car travel.

If you do not want to use a crate, you should still make sure your German Shepherd is safe in the car. Seatbelt harnesses (available from pet stores) will ensure your pup isn't loose in the car (which is dangerous both for him and for you).

SOCIALISATION

You should introduce your German Shepherd to as many new experiences and situations as you can, as soon as he is protected by his course of puppy vaccinations. As well as meeting all types of friendly people (men, women and children of different ages and cultures), he should be introduced to as many things as possible that he may later encounter – buses, trains, wheelchairs, prams, umbrellas, crash helmets, bicycles, rollerblades etc.

To us humans all these things are very familiar, and it is difficult to appreciate why it is so important to accustom the pup to something as harmless as a pair of sunglasses and a hat. But imagine if you had never seen these things before... Anything unfamiliar is unnerving, so introduce your pup to as much as possible while he is still a 'blank canvas', forming his impression of the world around him.

Household Appliances

A puppy raised in the home by a reputable breeder should be used to everyday household sounds. However, some noises (e.g. vacuum cleaner, washing machine) may need a little more work to get the puppy to accept them.

Aerosols (with their hissing sound) can be particularly startling for pups – especially as German Shepherds are so very noise-sensitive. To make sure your German Shepherd does not carry his aerosol phobia with him into adulthood, introduce him to the aerosol from a young age.

Accustom your puppy to as many different experiences as possible, so he learns he has nothing to fear from everyday sights and sounds.

- When the pup is relaxed, ask someone to spray an aerosol for just an instant in another room. (It is a good excuse to encourage someone to do the dusting for you!)
- Ignore the sound, and encourage the pup to do the same by distracting him with a toy and some treats.
- When he stops reacting to the sound, the same exercise can take place in the room where the puppy is. Do not give a treat when he reacts to the sound, but do give one when he ignores it.
- Eventually, he will learn that no harm comes of the sound. Do not use aerosol flea treatments on him until he has fully overcome his nervousness. Opt for alternative, silent treatments, such as pump sprays or spot-ons instead. (Always read the manufacturer's guidelines; if you have any queries, consult your vet.)

Happy To Be Handled

Your puppy should learn to be friendly to everyone. German Shepherds bond so closely with their owners that there is a danger that, unless they are properly socialised, they can become overprotective of the owner and suspicious of everyone else. A pup's capacity to love and to be loved has no boundaries, and he will give and take affection from all and sundry. You must encourage your German Shepherd to keep this carefree, trusting attitude so that he grows into a good-tempered adult. He is still likely to give a warning bark when someone approaches the house – such is his natural guarding instinct – but you must never encourage your dog to be aggressive, or you will have a real problem on your hands.

Your puppy should be handled by a variety of people well into his adulthood. Anyone should be able to touch him all over, check his teeth and ears, groom him, and so on. This

It is important that your puppy gets used to being handled.

will make life considerably easier when he needs to be examined by the vet, groomed professionally, or assessed by a judge in the show ring. It will also make him a nicer pet to share your life with.

TRAINING YOUR SHEPHERD

The German Shepherd's trust and loyalty is something that you must earn. He will bond closely not with the person who feeds him, but with the person who trains him. He won't turn his nose up at a treat or a toy bribe, and, if properly socialised, will be affectionate to all his friends, family and acquaintances, but he will truly *respect* his trainer.

In the initial stages of training, it helps if you put your Shepherd on a lead, so you should get him used to wearing a collar from as early as possible. Distract his attention away from the collar by giving him treats or playing a game with a new toy when the collar is first put on.

Putting a lead on a pup for training sessions can be compared to putting a child in a school uniform – it is a symbol to the dog that 'this is learning time'. It shouldn't signal the end of fun (training won't work unless the dog enjoys it), but it should help to focus your dog's mind. Plus, of course, it helps you to remain in control of your dog in the initial stages when he is still getting the idea of what is expected of him.

Pups are never too young to learn. Short training sessions introducing them to the basics should be started when you first get the pup home at about eight weeks. It will save a lot of

MOTIVATION

The key to training your German Shepherd Dog is to work out what makes him tick. Yes, he'll work for treats or for a toy, but his main motivation is to please you.

Originally bred to work for and with people, the German Shepherd lives to work and to serve – whether that is herding sheep or fetching his owner's slippers.

A cuddle and a 'Good boy' mean the world to him.

He never needs to be shouted at or treated harshly. For him, being ignored by his owner (i.e. not receiving praise or a treat) is punishment enough, and he will do his utmost to win back his owner's praise and esteem.

At the end of every training session, practise a couple of exercises that the dog finds easy. Finish with a game with your dog's favourite toy, so that he always leaves a training session having had some success and a lot of fun.

---

work in the long run – a young pup will soon pick up what is expected (certainly by about 16 weeks) and will be much easier to teach than a large, unmannered six-month-old who has never had a day's training in his life.

Recall

Teaching your German Shepherd to come when called is one of the first things you should do, and it should be continued into his adulthood. In many breeds, recall can be very difficult, but it is not generally too much of a problem with the German Shepherd. Most do not venture too far from their owners when out walking.

To make sure it does not become a problem, however, invest some of your training time in recall when the pup is still young and impressionable.

Stage One

• Ask a friend to hold the pup. Sit a short distance in front of him, and call him over by his name. Be as excited as possible, to show him that you really want to be with him.

Make yourself sound really exciting so that your puppy really wants to come to you.

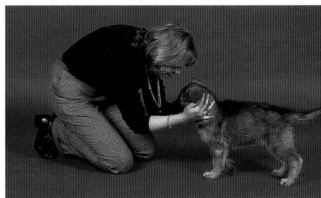

Reward with plenty of praise.

- When your puppy reaches you, praise him, and have a game or give him a treat so he learns that coming to you is worth the effort.
- If your puppy doesn't come to you, it is because you are not being interesting enough – work on your tone of voice, tap your hands on the floor, wave a toy at him, etc.
- Increase the distance between the two of you, until you can call him from another room to you, or from the garden to you, and he will reliably come.

Stage Two

- When your German Shepherd is fully inoculated, take him out to the park on a long or extending lead, and call him back to you throughout your time there. Give a treat and lots of fuss every time he comes, then send him off to play again.
- If he doesn't come, give a gentle tug on the line to encourage him to come to you. If he still refuses, bring him in on the line, shortening the line gently and slowly. You will then need to practise on a lead (see Stage One). Gradually increase the length of the lead/line.
- When you are sure that he will reliably come when called, practise off the lead.
- Never chase after your pup when he doesn't come. To a fun-loving pup, playing chase is a wonderfully enjoyable game and he will never come to you if he thinks his refusal will result in cat-and-mouse around the park. If he doesn't come, turn around and walk away from him. You will be surprised at how

TRAINING TIP

Use your German Shepherd's name as much as possible when training, particularly before a training command. Saying the name will help to focus the dog's attention, in time to receive the command. It is particularly useful if you are training in a class environment, or if you have (or plan to have) other dogs.

quickly he will come running to you if he thinks he is seriously being ignored or left behind!
- Remember that the whole family should practise the exercise – or *you* will be stuck with dog-walking duties for the whole of the dog's life!

Sit

This is one of the most important exercises – and one of the simplest. Having a dog that will reliably sit in a number of situations will make life much easier for you. Many people are intimidated by German Shepherds because of their size and past bad publicity, so it is important to be able to control your dog and for him to sit quietly when told. This isn't just a case of good manners, but is also important for the public perception of the breed. If your German Shepherd is a good ambassador, it may encourage people to reconsider their prejudices.
- Show your Shepherd pup a really tasty treat with the other hand and give him just a taste of it to get him eager.

- Show him the treat again so that he will follow it with his head and try to take it.
- Hold the treat just above his head and then move your hand back towards his neck, so that the pup has to stretch up and lean back to reach it.
- He will almost be in the Sit position, but you will have to move your hand back just a fraction so that he must put his bottom on the floor to reach up for the treat.
- As soon as he sits, say "Sit" and give him the treat he has worked so hard for.
- After a few practices, he will understand what he needs to get the treat, and the exercise will become easier and easier. Eventually, the word "Sit" will be sufficient to put him in position.
- It is also useful, outside training sessions, to say "Sit" whenever you see the pup sitting down of his own accord. That way, he will learn to associate the word with the action.

- Ask him to sit before you give him his meal, before walking through doors, while meeting people etc. It will not only make life easier for you, it will also help to keep the exercise fresh in the dog's mind.

Down

The Down is taught in the same way as the Sit – encouraging the dog into position by the careful positioning of a hand and a treat. Once he is familiar with the Sit exercise, your bright German Shepherd will catch on very quickly to what is expected of him for this exercise, too.

- Put your pup in the Sit position.
- Show him a treat in your hand, putting it quite close to his face, and then put your hand on the floor a little way in front of him. This will encourage him to follow the treat with his head, until his head is on the floor.
- Make sure you hold the treat in such a way

 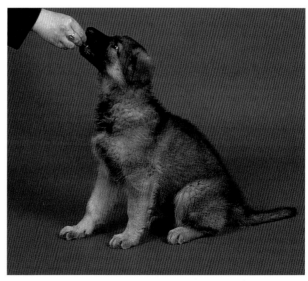

If a treat is held above the puppy's head, he will look up and naturally lower himself into the Sit position.

Lower the treat down to the floor, and your puppy will follow his nose and go into the Down position.

that a little of it is showing, but that you still have firm control of it so that he cannot take it unless you allow him to.

- If he gets too excited, he will break the Sit, but this isn't a disaster. He will try to get the treat by standing up but at the same time stooping down, and will eventually realise that, to get closer to it, he will have to lie down. As soon as he does so, say "Down", praise him and give him the treat.
- German Shepherds do not give up easily, but if your pup gets fed up trying to get the treat without working out that he has to get down on the floor to it, show him the treat and give him just a tiny amount so that his interest is reawakened.
- As with the Sit, incidental training is very useful. Every time you see your pup lie down, say "Down" and praise him (he will be a little confused by this, but it works!).

Stay

German Shepherds are renowned for wanting to be with their owners the majority of the time (it is no surprise that there are so many called Shadow), so this exercise can be a little trickier than the previous two. However, if you take things slowly, starting with very short stays at a close distance, your pup won't think he is being deserted. It is also important to teach the pup

that you *always* come back, and that there will be lots of love and affection when you do. His confidence will grow and he will soon learn that you are well worth waiting for.

- Put your German Shepherd on a lead, put him in the Sit position and firmly tell him to "Stay", while putting your arm out in front of you, with your palm facing the dog.
- Take just one step back, wait a second, then step up to him again, give him a treat, a cuddle and lots of adulation.
- Over the practice sessions, increase the number of steps away from your dog and the length of time taken before returning to him. As you can take more steps, exchange the lead for a long training line.
- Once he has mastered this, practise putting the lead or line on the floor and walking around your dog in a circle. If you can see he is becoming restless, remind him to "Stay".

The Stay exercise should be built up in gradual stages.

TRAINING TIP

Short, five-minute training sessions practised a few times a day are far more effective than a whole afternoon's training once a week.

- If he breaks a Stay, calmly put him back in a Sit. Do not shout or lose your temper; just do not give the treat or praise him. When you try again, go down a level. For example, if your dog broke a 15-second Stay at 10 paces, then go back to practising a 10-second Stay at 6 paces. Only when he has really conquered each level should you consider increasing the difficulty.

Lead-training

A light puppy-collar will help your German Shepherd to get used to wearing something around his neck. If your dog is tattooed or microchipped, it is still important that he wears a collar with your contact details on the tag. This will ensure that he can be returned to you immediately if found (without having to seek out somewhere that has a scanner to read the chip, etc.).

As well as being important for identification purposes, a collar is essential for lead-walking. Before you start lead-training, your German Shepherd pup must be perfectly happy to wear a collar.

Practise in the garden at first. When he has had his inoculations, take him out to a public area.

- Put your pup on your left-hand side, with his front legs parallel with yours.
- Hold the lead in your right hand; your left hand can hold any dangling excess lead, and a treat or a toy. This hand should be held just above your stomach.
- Take a step forward (leading off with your left foot) and encourage the dog to walk forward too, by saying his name, encouraging him verbally, and gently pulling on the lead. Show him the treat/toy in your left hand and encourage him to follow it.
- If he is distracted, call his name, squeak a toy, or show him a treat, so that he will be focused on you and will walk beside you. Your dog should be attentive to you. He should watch your face and ignore all other distractions. Say his name if his concentration strays.
- When he is walking well beside you, say "Heel" and encourage him with a calm voice – being too excited will encourage him to jump up at you. Stop after a short distance and give him a treat.
- If he steams ahead, do not hurry after him; instead, stop in your tracks, gently tug the lead, and call him back to you. Put him in the Sit position and start again. Stopping, turning around and walking in the other direction also works. If your pup realises you are unpredictable, he will be keen to walk closer to you in future.
- If he is walking too far out from your leg, you can tell him "In" and gently tug on the lead to bring him in closer to you. The

To start with, a treat or a toy may be needed to encourage your puppy to walk forward on the lead.

Every time your German Shepherd barks when you do not want him to, tell him to be "Quiet". Do not shout or be aggressive in the command; you should be as professional as if you were telling the dog to "Sit". Shouting will increase the dog's nervousness and will make him bark even more. He will believe that you are also 'barking' at the passer-by, the postman, or next door's cat, and that he is therefore justified to do so.

If he will not be quiet when commanded, drop some training discs or your keys on the floor. The unexpected sound will silence him for a moment. Immediately praise him for being quiet.

moment he is in the correct position again, give lots of praise.

• When he is walking in the correct way, start walking in large left-hand and right-hand circles. When he is really attentive to you, introduce sharper turns to the left and right to keep him on his toes.

Quiet

German Shepherds can be noisy, particularly when they feel they have to defend their property. Their vocal nature relates to their watchdog origins where they would have to bark to alert their master of the approach of strangers or predators and to drive them away. It is important that your German Shepherd does not become territorial about your property. Once unleashed, the instinct becomes stronger and stronger, and can get out of hand.

Puppy Classes

Once your German Shepherd pup has been to a few puppy parties, and is socialised with other dogs and people, you should enrol at a basic obedience class. Teaching him to sit, go down, stay, come and walk on the lead in a controlled manner is easy enough when taught in the home where there are few distractions, but is an entirely different matter in the outside world. If your German Shepherd will obey you when surrounded by a roomful of playful, noisy

TRAINING TIP

Once you choose a command word (such as "Sit", "Down", "Stay", etc.), keep it short and simple, and stick to it. Even slight changes, such as "Sit down" can confuse a dog. Is he meant to sit or to lie down?

puppies, then you will be in with a fighting chance of controlling him in a park situation.

It is vitally important to find the right training class. All dogs need careful handing, but it is especially important with the German Shepherd. He might appear big and boisterous, but he is a very sensitive dog whose spirit can be broken very easily with unkind handling. German Shepherds are so intelligent; they do not need tough, rough discipline – no dog does. They are so tuned in to their owners that they generally know from the tone of voice when they have done wrong or right.

Visit several classes before enrolling. Do not take your German Shepherd along; instead, sit and watch how the other dogs are treated. Would you be happy if your dog was taught the same way? Are fair and effective reward-based methods used, rather than discipline based on fear and punishment? If you are at all unhappy with the methods used, try another class.

Limiting Exercise

Many people think that, because the adult German Shepherd is a big dog and needs considerable exercise, a puppy needs to be walked for miles and miles too. Overexercising a dog can be very harmful, especially with the German Shepherd, whose bones and joints need very careful management.

Controlled play in the garden is enough exercise for a German Shepherd pup, and, as he grows, lead-walking can be enjoyed too. He shouldn't have anything too energetic until his bones are grown and are stronger, at around one year of age. Jumping on and off furniture or using the stairs should also be discouraged.

Remember, too much exercise can do untold damage to joints while a puppy is growing.

CHAPTER THREE

THE ADOLESCENT GERMAN SHEPHERD DOG

Adolescence is a tough time for humans and dogs alike. Even with good rearing, some adolescent German Shepherds can try their owners' patience by becoming rebellious, apparently 'forgetting' their training and early education. Do not respond by becoming angry and infuriated. This is the time when your Shepherd needs to have consistent – but kind – discipline to help him re-establish his own identity and his status within the family.

With a breed as intelligent and complex as the German Shepherd, adolescence can be a particularly difficult time if the dog did not receive sufficient handling or training when a pup. The most successful way of dealing with problems is to prevent them, so socialise your pup thoroughly (Chapter Two) to give him the best start in life.

However, if your German Shepherd has become a terrible teenager despite your best efforts, or if you took on an adolescent from another home, you will have to do some serious trouble-shooting to prevent 'a phase' turning into a lifetime habit.

Possessiveness

German Shepherds were bred to guard, so it should come as no surprise to learn that the breed can become over-possessive of toys, food or people if this inherent trait is left unchecked. If a Shepherd has real respect for his owners (resulting from kindness and from consistent discipline), he would not dream of attempting to assert his superiority, and so would not counter claims to his food bowl, his toys, or his bed. However, a dog that is owned by a weak, unconfident handler, may decide to challenge the hierarchy. In such a situation, no-go areas develop where the dog will not tolerate having his 'possessions' interfered with.

To prevent this happening, show your dog that you always have the right to his things (Chapter Two). However, if a problem has

already become established, you will have to deal with it. If your German Shepherd is possessive of a certain toy, you need to divest the object of its special significance.

If, for example, your Shepherd is obsessed with a tennis ball, a behaviourist may advise that you buy 20 and give them all to him in one go. In some circumstances, this may result in the ball losing its appeal. It can be more successful than simply removing the toy (as this course of action confirms the dog's initial instinct that he was right to guard the toy all along). Bowl guarding can be treated in the same way – pouring his dried food all over the kitchen floor weans the dog off the bowl's significance.

This is fine as far as it goes, but all you are really doing is managing the problem, not solving its underlying cause, and this type of treatment cannot be used for all types of possession. The causes can be many and varied, but most often over-possessiveness is the result of dominance (see below), or of insecurity (if, for example, a new dog has been introduced into the household).

Remember, possessiveness/guarding can lead to serious aggression problems if left unchecked, so consult a professional dog trainer or animal behaviourist at the first sign of trouble.

Dominance

Dogs are pack animals that live by a social hierarchy. Those in the higher ranks of the hierarchy have responsibilities for providing for the pack (seeking food, finding shelter, imposing discipline, and enforcing mating rights). In return, they have more privileges than the lower-status dogs. Of course, the single pack leader has the most power.

Most dogs now live in a domestic environment, but they still interpret social behaviour in terms of their wild pack hierarchy. The owner has the same responsibilities as the canine pack leader, and so should be afforded the same respect from his subordinates (i.e. the dog). The owner/leader should be allowed to

• Go through doors first
• Be fed first

Do not allow your Shepherd to assert his dominance by breaking house rules.

Guarding behaviour can be regarded as a sign of self-assertion.

- Have access to any area of the house or garden
- Take any item that belongs to a member of his pack
- Be responsible for discipline.

Not allowing the dog to race up the stairs before his owner, or to sleep on his owner's bed may seem to be pedantic and unnecessary, but you should look at what these signals mean in canine terms. They are privileges that show the dog is more important than the pack leader.

Of course, if you want a dog to sleep on your bed, you should let him. After all, having a pet is not something that can be conducted by a rule book, every family is unique and may want different things from their dog. The key issue is that you must always be in control. Your Shepherd must obey you, and get off the bed or the sofa the moment you ask him to. If he doesn't, or worse, if he growls, seek professional advice immediately.

The signs of dominant behaviour may include

- Guarding items (bowls, chairs, toys), or areas of the house
- Attention-seeking (nudging, barking etc.)
- Refusal to accept grooming
- Holding eye contact for a prolonged period.

A dominant Shepherd will need to have his behaviour reshaped. It is your job to reassert your authority, by ensuring that your Shepherd is responsive to commands, and accepts his subservient role in the family 'pack'. There are a number of simple procedures to observe, such as feeding your dog after the family, and making sure he always goes through the door after you, which will help to define his status.

Reshaping

If you don't want your dog to go upstairs or to sleep on your bed, then bar him access to it. Shut the bedroom door, or invest in a stair-gate. If your Shepherd races through a door ahead of you, let him, but do not follow him through the door. He will be quite lost that he is separated from you, and, as soon as you open the door, he will race back to you. There may be times that you would like your Shepherd to walk in front of you – if you are carrying the shopping indoors, for example. If this is the case, tell him to walk through first. As before, it must be your decision, not the dog's.

If your dog's dominance manifests itself in aggression towards you, you must seek the advice of a qualified animal behaviourist.

A dog that barks persistently can be seen as threatening.

Barking

The German Shepherd was bred to guard and to protect, so it is natural for him to bark when someone approaches his territory. A warning bark is all very well, particularly if this is followed up by a warm welcome once you have opened the door and greeted the 'stranger' (see Chapter Two).

However, a dog that barks persistently can be seen as a threat, as well as being regarded as a social nuisance. In this case, you will need to start from scratch and re-educate your dog.

Quiet

Every time your dog barks inappropriately (e.g. gives more than a warning bark), tell him "Quiet". Give the command firmly, but do not shout, or you will get the dog overexcited. It is imperative that you are always consistent. For the training to work, you must tell him to be quiet every time he barks – without exception.

Training Discs

Once a dog starts barking, it can be difficult to stop him, as he gets more and more excited. The more you shout, the more excited and anxious he becomes. Dropping training discs (small metal circles shaped like mini-cymbals) or a bunch of keys can work to startle the dog out of his repetitive cycle of barking. The moment he stops, you can then praise him for being quiet, and keep him distracted with a quick game. All rewards must end the moment your dog starts barking again.

Distraction

One way of silencing your dog is to turn the dog's attention to something else. Tell him to "Sit", to fetch your slippers, etc. to distract him. He cannot bark while he is concentrating on obedience exercises.

Remember that it is natural for a dog to bark. Dogs bark to communicate, so you should not seek to stop him from ever 'speaking' again. If your dog's barking is more than simply telling you of someone's approach, or of warning the person away, you should investigate the cause behind it. Perhaps he is in pain, or is feeling insecure. If you are at all concerned, you should seek the services of a vet and/or professional trainer.

Herding/Chasing

Shepherding breeds have a well-developed instinct to chase. Modern-day living in pet homes often fails to satisfy the dog's powerful impulses, and, in the event of having no woolly things to chase, the dog may find alternative victims to herd – joggers, cyclists, skateboarders... if it moves, a frustrated Collie or German Shepherd will herd it.

This is a very complex problem that will need sensitive handling, so you should contact your vet or a professional dog trainer/behaviourist in the first instance. If it is not dealt with, your German Shepherd may start chasing motorcycles or cars, and many dogs have died in these circumstances. Manage the problem while you are seeking professional advice, by keeping your dog on an extending lead when out walking. You should also work on your dog's obedience, so that you can put him in a Down whenever a tempting chase situation presents itself.

Aggression

A well-reared, well-socialised German Shepherd puppy should grow up into a happy, well-behaved adult, without the slightest hint of aggression in him. However, German Shepherds are very sensitive dogs with long memories, and if your dog has been frightened by something, he could develop a phobia. For example, if your puppy has been set upon by a black Poodle, he may become frightened not only of Poodles, but of all black dogs – or, worse still, of all dogs he meets.

This fear may not just manifest itself in cowering behind you in the park, it can sometimes develop as fear-aggression, where the dog lashes out whenever faced with a potential aggressor, hoping that he can attack before being attacked.

Again, it is a question of going back to basics. Your German Shepherd needs to learn that interacting with dogs is good fun. Meeting and socialising with dogs of all shapes, sizes and colours will show him this, so contact your local dog trainer. Many trainers have 'stooge' dogs – dogs so well-behaved and well-socialised that they can be trusted never to react aggressively to other dogs. Contact of this kind will help to

Reprimand your Shepherd at the first sign of wanting to chase – and on every occasion when he shows undue interest in livestock – and this will help to prevent the instinct from developing.

build your German Shepherd's trust in his fellow canines, and can form a firm foundation for future contact with other dogs. Other dogs can then gradually be introduced under supervised control. A dog never cures itself of aggression; it is a problem that can only get worse, so you should seek professional advice immediately, particularly if the dog's aggression is directed towards people. Never fight fire with fire, or you can aggravate the problem. Always act calmly when dealing with your dog.

The well-socialised Shepherd will get on well with other dogs. Photo courtesy: Kari Selinger.

dogs of all breeds can act a little out of character, becoming more rebellious as a result of the hormones coursing through their veins.

Recall is one of the first areas to suffer, as the dog is more interested in following his nose (and other walkers and dogs) than being with his owner. And, like a child testing what he can get away with, your German Shepherd may become disobedient and unruly, testing his relationship with you.

It is essential that you do not tolerate any undesirable behaviour. If your Shepherd does not come back when he is called, you must make yourself more interesting so that he wants your company. Do not be embarrassed, even if you are in a busy park: jump up and down, and call in an excited voice. If this fails, try running in the opposite direction – few dogs can resist running to catch up. When your Shepherd

Recall

Generally, adult German Shepherds are great dogs to walk, rarely letting their owners out of their sight. Instead of galloping off and not being seen for the rest of the walk, many German Shepherds stick fairly closely to their owners. Adolescence, however, is a time when

returns to you, give lots of praise (even if it's between gritted teeth), so that he is rewarded for being with you. Never give up, believing you are fighting a losing battle and that your dog will eventually grow out of it. Your dog will take this as an open invitation for the uncorrected misbehaviour to become the norm.

Work hard to instil a good recall response from your German Shepherd while he is still a pup (see the exercises in Chapter Two). You will then have solid foundations with which to work.

• Find what really motivates your German Shepherd – be it a particular toy or a type of treat (liver or cheese are often favourites). Keep the reward in your pocket when you go out for a walk.

• Keep your German Shepherd on an extending lead and call him back to you at intervals throughout your walk together. Make yourself sound exciting, show the reward to him, and give it to him the moment he returns to you. Send him off to play as soon as he has had his treat.

• Do not let your Shepherd off the extending lead in an open area until you are certain he will come back. Until then, only train off the lead in your enclosed garden, or on a tennis court, or some other 'safe' area. When training off the lead, keep calling your Shepherd back for a treat, as before.

• If he has taken a long time to come back, never show your displeasure or frustration when he does finally return. Shouting at your dog will make him believe you are angry that he *came* back (not that he *wouldn't* come back), and will make him think twice about doing so in the future.

Neutering

Some behavioural problems can have an hormonal cause. Perhaps your male is too boisterous, is scent-marking, or is overly interested in the opposite sex. If your vet believes hormones are having a detrimental effect on your dog, he may advise you to have the dog neutered.

As well as having a positive effect on your dog's behaviour, neutering also has several health benefits, and may be worth considering if you do not intend to show your dog or breed from him/her. In bitches, removing the womb removes the chance of developing a pyometra (where the womb becomes infected with pus); this condition can be fatal if it is not caught in time. A reduced chance of mammary tumours is another considerable benefit from spaying. You will also be saved the inconvenience of dealing with seasons, and all

the complications of keeping other dogs away during this time. In males, the likelihood of prostate disorders are reduced following neutering.

Weight increase and coat changes are often cited as the disadvantages of neutering. However, keeping an eye on your dog's weight and adjusting the diet accordingly should prevent any unwanted increase. Coat changes are of little significance to those keeping their dogs as pets; those involved in the show world are less likely to neuter in the first place.

The age at which a dog or bitch is neutered varies according to the vet's individual preferences. Some vets neuter as early as 18 weeks; some advise waiting until the dog has matured sexually or until the bitch has had her first season. Talk to your own vet about your particular circumstances to see what he or she advises.

CHAPTER FOUR

THE FAMILY DOG

The German Shepherd loves tending to his family flock, sharing his life with them, enjoying their company, and keeping an attentive eye on everyone's whereabouts and safety. When on a family walk, he is a real go-getter who makes the most of every minute he spends with his loved ones, enjoying life to the full.

HAPPY FAMILIES

Adaptable, loyal and loving, the German Shepherd is an asset to most families. He tends to bond more closely with one person, and, if not properly socialised and handled, he can be overprotective of his 'chosen one'. However, if raised sensibly, your German Shepherd's close bond with his favourite will not be to the detriment of others, and he should enjoy close relationships with other family members, friends and acquaintances.

The German Shepherd loves to be part of family activities.

BIG-KID RUSS

Philamena McCarthy has always kept German Shepherds, but she was anxious that no-one's nose should be out of joint with the arrival of her grandchildren.

"Russ, my seven-year-old German Shepherd, is beautiful to look at. He is handsome and big, and sweet-natured," says Philamena. "He was interested in my granddaughter Abigail even before she was born – he would sniff around my daughter's tummy, and we would say 'There's a baby in there.'

"When Abigail was born, we took Russ over to the carry-cot, he stuck his nose in it, and we took him outside to have a game. Then we took him in for another sniff, and so on. He's very protective of her now, and knows she is one of his family.

"Russ had never met a new-born baby before. When he was a puppy, he had met my niece's 18-month-old, but had never encountered a young baby. With subsequent grandchildren (18-month-old Sophie and three-year-old Siobhan), he just had a look in the carry-cot and seemed to say 'Oh,

that's another one, is it?' He adores them all, and they adore him.

"The children are always very careful around him, and have already learnt to be very respectful. They never pulled at his coat, even when they were crawling, and would always move carefully around him.

"Russ has a box of his own toys, and he never touches the children's. They hand-feed him and give him their yoghurt pots to lick out when they have finished with them. It's a very special relationship that children have with animals.

"My daughter's midwife gave some very good advice to her when the first baby was born. She said 'Always remember the dog was there first,' and we have been careful to make sure Russ is as much an integral part of our family as he always was. He has never been jealous of the attention we give to the children, and the children are now old enough to give him treats when they come, so he is always delighted when they come round!"

Russ: A natural guardian of the children.

The German Shepherd loves family activities, and hates to be excluded. This is not a dog that particularly enjoys his own company, believing it is his duty to watch and to check on his family, for whom he feels very responsible.

On a country walk, for example, the owner/dog roles are likely to be reversed. Instead of you calling and chasing after your dog, the daily routine of many long-suffering owners, you will probably find that your German Shepherd will stick close by, preferring to keep a close eye on you. You shouldn't take this for granted, though, and should still ensure that you have good recall control over him – he has a keen nose on him, and may pick up an interesting scent that takes him off.

To use his natural scenting ability and to spice up your walks together, you might like to start training your German Shepherd to track.

- While he is still young and walking on a lead, drop a glove, stop a very short distance on, and ask your dog to "Find it!".
- At first, your pup is likely to be bemused by this request and will fail to understand what is expected of him.
- Walk close to the glove, and if the puppy shows any interest in it at all, praise him like mad, give him a treat, and make him feel especially clever.
- Again, he is likely to be rather confused, but will nevertheless enjoy the fuss, and will be keen to 'find' something for you again in the future.
- Gradually extend the distance between

dropping an item and asking your German Shepherd to "Find it".

This exercise is good fun, exercises your dog's mind as well as his body, and is very useful when you come to lose something you really did not intend to.

Swimming is another activity that many German Shepherds enjoy. If controlled, it can be a good form of exercise, as it does not put excessive pressure on the joints. You must make sure that your Shepherd is not allowed to swim in cold water for prolonged periods, and he must be thoroughly dried afterwards.

RESCUE DOGS

Because they are such popular dogs, numerically strong both sides of the Atlantic, it is no surprise that German Shepherds also have a high presence in the rescue centres. Pet German Shepherds are sensitive dogs that love and need contact with their owners; they do not generally thrive in a rescue kennel environment.

The number of German Shepherds in rescue would be significantly fewer if owners had been properly informed about the breed from the start. Some people buy a German Shepherd as a guard dog, with little consideration for the dog's basic exercise and training needs. Left out in the back garden all day, with little human contact, the dog becomes increasingly territorial, aggressive and destructive. If you want your property protected, buy an alarm, not a highly intelligent living creature.

A NEW START

Kari Selinger has been rescuing and rehoming dogs for Michigan German Shepherd Rescue for six years. She fosters dogs for the rescue organisation, and has anything up to three foster or rescue German Shepherds in her home at any one time.

"Living with a rescue German Shepherd can be very rewarding. They seem to know they are rescued and that they have a second chance in life.

"There are often minor challenges with rescuing a German Shepherd Dog. If they were not properly socialised, they may be a little fearful and not very confident. Often, they have been left outside or constantly confined to a crate. So house-breaking (house-training) is an issue.

"One dog in particular is Hana, who was rescued from a dreadful situation – a backyard puppy-mill (puppy-farm). She spent her first three years living outside in extreme temperatures. They used her as a brood bitch from the age of six months old; when she was

rescued, she had just had 10 pups. There were several breeds of dogs at the mill, including Siberian Huskies, Dalmatians, Border Collies, Miniature Pinschers... basically breeding pairs of many types of dog. The dogs were standing in faeces up to their hocks, and were just tossed food.

Hana spent the first three years of her life living outside; her contact with people was minimal.

"When Hana and the others were rescued, they had no idea what walking on a leash was, had never been in a car, and had never climbed stairs. They didn't know what to do with food- or water-bowls, didn't know how to play, and had never been petted... all the basics in a happy dog's life.

"In foster care, we watched Hana improve. At first she would hit the deck as if she was going to be beaten when we threw a ball for the other dogs; now she playfully romps when the ball is tossed. Climbing stairs was interesting. She was absolutely fearful. Several times she was carried down the stairs and then we coaxed her up the stairs (climbing is generally easier than descending).

Animal aggression was never shown, but it was obvious that she lacked confidence and was uncertain in new surroundings.

"Patience was the key. We let Hana take it at her own pace. After about two months, she decided we were okay. The turning point was when she began to play with the other dogs and she started to bark and talk back to us. She first trusted the other dogs, then us.

"Basic obedience goes a long way, and, as smart and willing to please as she is, Hana quickly gained her confidence (she even gets cocky) and has continued beyond basic obedience to Open Competitive Obedience.

' Missi has taught me patience, persistence and the need for me to be consistent '

"Hana is a true ambassador for the breed. When people meet her on the street, she is reserved yet allows petting. This caution is a feature of the breed.

"She sees a new baby in the house as just an extension of her family – someone new to look after. My baby Joe was premature, and she seems to understand that he is even more delicate. She always keeps an eye on him; she just rests her head near his crib, calm and watchful.

"We have seen Hana blossom from a very reserved, sad, uncertain dog, into a loyal, fun-loving, confident, German Shepherd – and it has been a joy to watch. She has now been homed with a very dear friend of mine, Susan Schmidt. Sometimes we make very hard decisions, and that was one of them. Susan has been involved with Hana from the outset, and has been training her for her Companion Dog Obedience title. Susan has a son, Joe, and another dog, a GSD-Husky mix, and they absolutely adore

each other. Plus, I get to walk with Hana every day.

"Hana's story has a happy ending, but I am also going to share the story of Missi. She is probably the best German Shepherd I have ever owned and she represents a higher percentage of the type of dogs that come into rescue. Puppy-mill dogs and neglected dogs come in occasionally, but most of the dogs that end up in German Shepherd rescue are the victims of under-educated owners who should never have owned a Shepherd in the first place.

"Missi is a dominant female with a strong work-drive and extreme intelligence. She is the one in the litter that pet owners should avoid. It is these dominant dogs that get tossed around because the owners cannot house-break them – they run away, or they are too hyperactive. Believe me, Missi was all these things.

"Missi was very vocal, and would constantly talk back to you – she always had to have the last word. With her high work-drive, she would chase cats and other dogs, and, being confident, she would protect her property to the best of her ability. Nothing could enter her territory without her knowing about it and giving her opinion on it.

"Patience, patience, patience and training have created a dog and a partner I could not do without. It took six months of continued training. During this time she learned I would not give in and that we could reach a compromise. Soon after, she became crate-trained and on the way to being house-broken. She learned the 'Leave' command (so no more animal-chasing), and she now cuddles up with

A NEW START

the three cats that live in my house.

"Missi has earned an AKC Companion (CD) title, and we are on our way to earning CDX and Agility titles. She does initially bark, more in the hope of scaring away intruders than anything else, but if I say it is okay, she acts like a playful pup. She has always been very soft and sweet with all kids. Even though she is incredibly active – she hardly sits still unless asked to – with the children, she is very calm, and just lies there so that they can pet her. She is always on the go, but whenever kids are around, she lets them make the first move, and tolerates everything they do.

"Missi will stay with us forever. We have worked so hard together, I have never experienced such a bond with a dog. We may have negotiated the terms, but Missi will do anything for me. Sometimes I think she knows me better than I know myself.

Hard work and patience have paid off, and Missi now has a very special bond with her owner.

In fact, it would be very difficult to find an adoptive family for Missi. The owner would need to stay one step ahead of her, and continue with her training, or else she would take advantage of them and end up in need of rescue again.

"As soon as we get new foster dogs in our home, Missi must always tell them who's boss – under me, of course. She is never aggressive, just dominant.

"Working and living with rescue German Shepherds is very rewarding. Hana gives joy to my life, and I am happy to have made a difference to her life and to my friend's. Hana has helped Susan to feel confident; she protects her, and has helped Susan to trust again.

"Missi has taught me patience, persistence, and the need to be consistent. She also makes me laugh every day, and has shown me that nothing worth having is easy!

It is preferable to divide the daily ration into two meals.

The other main reason for dogs being given up for adoption is the owners' changing circumstances, particularly a marriage break-up, or a new baby coming into the family.

Just because a dog is in rescue does not mean that it deserves to be there. Some people never consider taking on a rescue, believing the dogs must have done something terrible to be there in the first place. This is not usually the case. Most dogs are homeless through no fault of their own and, in time, adapt well to their new families.

Most rescue centres will give the dog a thorough physical and behavioural assessment. Provided the dog is not a stray, they will also have the dog's history. All this information will be used to see whether the dog is suited to your circumstances.

If you are interested in adopting a German Shepherd, contact your nearest rescue centre. Your national breed club will also have details of breed rescue schemes.

CARING FOR THE ADULT GSD
Feeding

A healthy diet is a significant part of caring for your German Shepherd. Being a large dog, it is important that he has the right 'fuel' to keep him in the peak of health.

The pet-food market offers a wide selection of foods to suit every breed, age-group, budget and taste. Some people prefer to feed the traditional 'meat and biscuits' diet, others opt for the hassle-free 'complete' foods. Although many dogs seem to prefer tinned meat, most complete foods are also eaten with relish, and offer the security of mind that your dog is receiving a diet that is nutritionally complete.

Every German Shepherd owner should be aware of bloat, which is seen in many of the larger breeds of dog. It is a potential killer, and you should be aware of the early warning signs to be in with a chance of saving your dog. Your dog will appear restless, often after eating. He may try to vomit. His stomach will feel very hard and will eventually bloat. The stomach twists, and blocked gases cannot escape. The dog should be taken to a vet without delay, or he can die very quickly.

To avoid the risk of bloat, take the following precautions:
- Never feed your dog immediately before or after exercise.
- Try to discourage him from gulping his food (and thereby taking in air). Putting a brick or a large ball in your dog's feeding bowl slows down fast-eaters (but make sure it is large enough not to be swallowed).
- Split the ration into two meals, rather than feeding a large quantity once a day.

See page 126 for more information on this condition.

Obesity

Obesity is a killer of any breed of dog, but can cause untold problems in the Shepherd, whose vulnerable joints cannot cope with the excess burden. Obesity also puts strain on the heart. Since coronary problems are present in some dogs in the breed, you are asking for trouble if you let your athletic German Shepherd become a dumpy couch-potato.

Obesity can be a particular difficulty if you train your Shepherd with treats. Use only tiny pieces of treat to give your dog a taste and to leave him eager for more. Remember that a small slice of raw carrot is often a welcome treat in day-to-day training – and you can then save the unhealthy sausage/cheese rewards for the occasional times when you really need the very best from your dog (in competitions, for example).

Exercise

As a large dog from a working origin, the healthy, adult German Shepherd is not content with a quick walk around the block. Muscle tone must be built up and then maintained. An ideal way of doing this is to find a stream and allow your Shepherd to walk up-stream against the current – but this option is not available to many. However, walking over uneven terrain has the same effect, giving your Shepherd the opportunity to use his body, concentrating on balance and co-ordination. Free-running is a good way of getting rid of excess energy, but you must find a suitable, safe environment.

The average owner will struggle to keep up with a Shepherd, a dog bred to have tremendous stamina. However, drawing on his natural instincts to retrieve is a good way of spicing up your exercise sessions together. When playing 'retrieve', always consider your dog's safety. Never throw sticks, or balls that are too small. Both can get lodged down the throat, and can cause great damage to your dog.

Although it is important that your German Shepherd gets enough exercise, it is equally vital that you do not overdo it. Shepherds never know when to stop. Unlike some breeds that will just sit down when they have had enough, the German Shepherd will never 'give in' and can seriously damage his joints by overexertion. It is important to build up his exercise gradually, and always to consider his well-being.

It is especially important to monitor the exercise of your older dog. Although he may look as if he can cope with the huge hikes he enjoyed when younger, perhaps your veteran Shepherd is really struggling to keep up, and his pride won't let him stop. (See page 58.)

Mental Stimulation

The German Shepherd needs mental activity just as much as physical activity. He is a highly intelligent dog that is not happy to stagnate indoors all the time. He needs to be kept occupied to avoid behavioural problems from developing. German Shepherds love training, so consider getting involved in Competitive Obedience, Agility, Working Trials etc. (See Chapter Five).

EXERCISING YOUR GERMAN SHEPHERD
**The athletic German Shepherd thrives on exercise –
and the more variation you can provide, the better he will like it.**

You can also keep your Shepherd on his toes by bringing his training into your everyday life. Ask him to Sit or to Speak before you give him his meal. Get him to go Down and Roll-over on a towel after coming back from a muddy walk, and so on. A trained dog is a happy dog – and you will find that working with your German Shepherd strengthens your relationship with him and brings you closer together.

Regular grooming is required, particularly when the coat is shedding.

GROOMING

Bathing
The Shepherd does not require much bathing. During moulting, however, it can be useful to loosen the dead coat. Bathe him in warm water (make sure he is on a non-slip surface), and be careful not to get any water in the eyes or ears. When your Shepherd is thoroughly wet, apply a gentle dog shampoo, and work into a lather. Make sure all detergent is rinsed away, and that he is dried carefully afterwards.

Brushing
The German Shepherd is a moulting (shedding) breed, so regular daily brushing is required. The equipment necessary includes:
- A slicker brush (used mainly on long-coats but is also useful when the normal-coated dog is moulting)
- A rake-type comb (metal)
- A good bristle brush
- A piece of velvet cloth.

Step-By-Step
- To start grooming, first brush the coat the wrong way with the slicker brush to loosen any dead hair.
- Then, with the rake, comb the hair the way it lies, starting at the back of the head.
- When you have removed as much of the dead coat as possible, brush the hair vigorously with the bristle brush.
- Pay special attention to the tail and trousers (the long hair on the rear of the hind legs), as dead hair tends to mat in these areas.
- Give the coat a final polish with the velvet cloth.

ROUTINE CARE

General Checks
After returning from a walk with your German Shepherd you should take a few minutes to check him over. Check his paws to remove any small stones or grass seeds that may have become embedded in his pads, or between his

toes, and remove any burrs from his ears and coat (pay particular attention to his belly).

Once or twice a week, when grooming your dog, give him a thorough check-over for any lumps or bumps, or anything else out of the ordinary, and contact your vet if you are at all concerned. It is particularly important to check your German Shepherd's bottom regularly, as the breed is prone to a nasty condition called anal furunculosis (see Chapter Eight). Because of the way the tail is held, the condition can remain undetected for some time.

Ears

Because the German Shepherd has erect ears, which have good air circulation, he does not suffer from ear problems as badly as, for example, the long-eared spaniel breeds. Mites can still be an occasional problem, however, so regular checks are advisable, particularly for dark deposits in the ear caused by mites.

You can buy ear-cleaning solutions from your vet. Follow the instructions carefully, being especially careful not to push anything deep into the ear.

Nails

Check the nails regularly to see if they need trimming. If given sufficient exercise on both hard and soft terrain, it is unlikely that the nails will need clipping very often. In the event of them being too long, use guillotine-type clippers.

Be very careful when clipping your dog's nails. Because German Shepherds have dark

If nails grow too long, they will need to be trimmed.

nails, it can be difficult to see the 'quick', the blood supply. It is better to shave off small amounts at a time, so that you do not accidentally remove too much of the nail. Cutting the 'quick' will be very painful to your dog and may make him less amenable to having his nails cut or his paws touched in future.

Teeth

Hopefully, your German Shepherd will have been used to having his teeth cleaned regularly

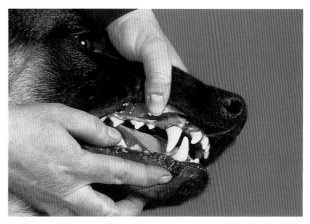

Check the teeth regularly: they will need to be cleaned if there is an accumulation of tartar.

from the time he was a puppy. If not, you will have to show him that a weekly brush is an enjoyable experience. Some people find that a fingerbrush (a brush that pops on the end of your finger) is easier to use than a conventional toothbrush. Use special meaty toothpaste designed for dogs (available from pet shops), place on a toothbrush or a fingerbrush and gently rub the teeth. End the session with a fun game to reward your dog for being so patient.

Long-coat Care

The long-coated German Shepherd needs more attention, as his coat mats much more readily than the normal coat. You should particularly check a long-coat's feet, and make a daily check between the toes and pads for any matted dirty hair. This can be removed by soaking in warm soapy water, and gently teasing it out with

If you have a long-coated Shepherd, you will have to work hard at keeping the coat free of tangles and mats.
Photo courtesy: Valerie Egger.

fingers and thumb. Dry the foot well on a towel.

The area behind the ears is another area that needs to be checked regularly for matted hair. These can be removed by teasing the mat away with your finger and thumb, and by gently using the slicker brush. In severe cases, it may be necessary to split the mat first with a pair of scissors. This should be done by cutting down the mat lengthways, not across it.

VETERAN CARE

Because of their working ability, German Shepherds generally have a good level of fitness and health, and many remain active well into old age. If you are unfortunate enough to have a dog which suffers from one of the degenerative conditions to which the breed is prone (hip dysplasia, CDRM – chronic degenerative radiculomyelopathy, etc.), his mobility may be affected by the time he reaches old age. However, this is not to say that the dog's quality of life is always compromised. You may have seen a veteran or two racing around in a 'cart', with wheels supporting the dog's back end. Many dogs adapt incredibly well to such contraptions. Modern veterinary medicine can also work wonders, so contact your vet for advice on how to make your Shepherd's life as comfortable as possible.

Even if your German Shepherd is in the peak of health, he will have different needs as a veteran. He may be slower than in his younger days, and will generally need gentle, less strenuous, exercise. Because he is likely to be less

KANE'S CASE

Valerie Egger has had very long-lived dogs. One of her most recent was Kane, who died recently, aged 15 years. Kane's father was 16 when he died. So what is the secret to having golden oldie German Shepherds?

"I think the predisposition to living a long life may be hereditary," says Valerie, who has been involved in the breed for nearly 60 years. Of course, preventive care, diet and lifetime care are also key factors in longevity.

"I was brought up in France until I was 15, and that was where we had our first Shepherd. He was grey, and very leggy. This was just after World War One, and there weren't many Shepherds around, only the ones that had been left behind after the Germans went back home. They were not very good specimens and didn't have the best temperaments.

"I have had a number of breeds throughout my life. The trouble is, it's difficult not to compare them against the German Shepherd. Compared to the Shepherd, other breeds can seem quite dim!

"I lost Kane soon after Christmas last year. His lines go back to 1942, and he had three German imports in his line. He had a good working temperament, and three of his sons have qualified as police dogs. Unlike some breeds, who start ageing at six years old, my Shepherds don't start showing their age until they are 10 or 11.

Kane's memory lives on in his grandson, Casey.

"Gradually, they slow up a bit, and may become a little wobbly on their back legs. With Kane, though, I can honestly say I didn't notice any change in him at all until three months or so before he died. His back legs started failing, but in the end he died in his sleep from heart and kidney failure.

"Because they become more affectionate and 'clingy' in their old age, it can make it more difficult when you do finally lose them. Kane had lots of character; he was playful, and liked to play the clown. He was like that until the day he died. It is comforting that he died peacefully, and it makes it a little easier to cope with the loss.

"It is some consolation that I still have contact with Kane through his grandson, who has some of his physical characteristics, and much of his personality. Like Kane, Casey is very friendly and eager to please. Breeding to a pattern, as I do, means none of the dogs are lost forever – their characteristics continue through the pedigree."

Kane: A very special companion.

Shepherds generally live to a ripe old age – but it is important that you adjust to their changing needs.

active, his diet will need adjusting. He will need less food, and a new balance of nutrients.

Older German Shepherds generally need less protein, phosphorus and sodium, and may need larger amounts of zinc, some vitamins, essential fatty acids and amino acids. Using a complete food specially formulated for veterans takes the complication out of catering for your dog's needs. If you do not wish to feed a complete food, talk to your vet about how you can best provide your German Shepherd with the nutrients he needs.

It is very important that you do not allow your German Shepherd to become obese. Living with him, it is very easy not to notice the gradual weight increase until it becomes a problem, so make an effort to weigh him regularly to keep it in check.

Spoiling your dog in his old age may be intended as an act of kindness, but could seriously damage your dog's health. There are other ways to pamper him in his twilight years than to overfeed him. Remember that he is actually likely to need *fewer* calories at this sedentary stage in his life.

If your dog is overweight, contact your vet surgery. Many hold special 'weigh-in' clinics and advice sessions, especially for portly pets and their concerned owners.

Your German Shepherd is likely to need more sleep. Some may crave more cuddles and contact, others may want to be alone more. He may be a little less patient than usual, so make sure he has his own space, somewhere to which he can escape if overly bothered by youngsters – either human or canine.

Don't forget to keep a closer eye on your veteran's nails, too. If he is exercising less, his nails may not be wearing down as they should, so may need trimming.

Euthanasia

One of the great sadnesses in life is that pets do not live as long as we do. After sharing your life with a Shepherd for 12 years or more, a very close bond will have developed, and it will be difficult to come to terms with saying goodbye.

If your vet has tried everything to cure or ease your dog's illness or condition, and he is still in pain or his quality of life is reduced, the vet will discuss with you the option of euthanasia. This is a painless way of putting your dog to sleep and of ending any suffering.

LETTING GO

Meg, a beautiful sable German Shepherd Dog, was the adored pet of Joan and John Brown from Portmahomack, Ross-shire, Scotland. Joan had a Wire Fox Terrier when she was a child, but Meg was the first dog in their married life. This, Joan believes, made them utterly unprepared for dealing with their grief when Meg died nine years later.

"We got Meg when she was 18 months old. She had a very good pedigree and was intended as a show dog, but it didn't work out. She was a very intelligent dog; she soon got bored by the tedium of showing, so her career was short-lived.

"Meg was always full of energy and was very protective. If John was out walking her and someone else started walking near him, she would race back to John and walk right beside him until the other person passed – then off she would go again.

"About a year before we lost Meg, we noticed something was wrong. On one of her walks, she just sat down. Normally she would do that if she had a thorn in her pads, or a small stone, and she would lift up the paw for John to remove the offending object. But she didn't lift her paw, and there was nothing there, so John had to carry her half a mile home. When he stopped to have a rest (she was 33 kgs/73lbs) and to get the circulation back in his arms, she started walking again. We now think that incident was the start of her CDRM (Chronic degenerative radiculomyelopathy).

"Eventually the condition got worse. Her steps became smaller, and she would shuffle rather than walk.

"The vet gave Meg some tablets to ease her condition, and they helped for a time, but soon she became much worse. We had to get her on her feet when she wanted to get up, and had to hand-feed her because she couldn't stand up and eat. When she couldn't move her head or wag her tail (CDRM affects the spine), we knew we couldn't carry on like this any more. It was obvious Meg was upset by her condition – you could see the sadness in her eyes.

"We took her back to the vet, who said there was nothing else that could be done. John and I were both in tears, she was such a lovely dog.

"We had her cremated at a lovely animal crematorium in Lincolnshire. Her ashes were scattered in their garden of remembrance and a plaque was placed there. We also had a plaque to take home to put in the garden.

"Our friends were all very supportive, and sent us comforting cards and flowers. Everyone who met Meg, loved her. She was a real treasure.

"Meg died five years ago, and we still miss her terribly. Every year, on the anniversary of her death, we have a little ceremony for her. We have a 'Meg corner' in the house, with her portrait and lots of photos, and we put some flowers there for her.

"People say 'Get another dog.' If we were younger, perhaps; but we are both in our mid-70s, and we don't really have enough energy to look after a young German Shepherd again.

"My advice for anyone who has faced the decision to euthanase a pet, is never to let the animal suffer. You are the guardian of your pet's welfare, and you take on that responsibility when you first take your puppy home. It does take some guts, and you should prepare to be shattered, but, sadly, losing a pet is an inescapable fact of owning one."

CHAPTER FIVE

BROADENING HORIZONS

The German Shepherd Dog is one of those breeds that needs a hobby. He is athletic and intelligent, and thrives when asked to do a job – whether that is fetching your slippers, running an Agility course, or performing Heelwork to Music. Your dog's potential will really be wasted if you don't exercise his mind as well as his body, so pick a doggie sport you will enjoy sharing with your Shepherd and sign up. Here are some ideas...

CANINE GOOD CITIZEN

The 'Good Citizen' scheme is an excellent starting point if you want to expand on your dog's initial puppy training. The American Kennel Club's Canine Good Citizen Program and the British Kennel Club's Good Citizen Dog Scheme encourage responsible pet ownership and educate dog owners about the benefits of having a well-behaved pet.

Your German Shepherd shouldn't find the tests too much of a challenge, provided you have trained and socialised him properly. The tests aim to produce well-mannered canine citizens, so the dogs are examined on behaving well in everyday situations, including:
• Accepting handling and grooming
• Responding to basic obedience commands
• Meeting another dog
• Walking on a loose lead in a controlled manner
• Walking confidently through a crowd of people
• Being approached and petted by a stranger.

If your German Shepherd needs to polish up his skills, see Chapter Two. There are many participating training clubs in the United Kingdom and the United States where you can enrol to prepare your dog for the tests. To find out more information on the schemes, contact your national Kennel Club.

Let your Shepherd progress at his own speed, and then he will grow in confidence.

AGILITY

Agility is one of the most popular canine sports, and it is easy to see why. Most dogs love racing round, tackling the obstacles – and both dog and owner keep very fit! Agility is a fun sport, especially for German Shepherds who are such quick and eager learners.

In Agility, the dog must tackle a series of obstacles in the correct order, within a set time and with no faults. The winning dog is the one that completes a clear round in the fastest time. A degree of basic obedience is required before starting. Your dog should be well behaved around other dogs, and you should have basic control over him, so that he won't just run off to play with one of his fellow pupils as soon as he is let off the lead.

Once you believe your German Shepherd is ready for training, join a local Agility club. This is the best place to learn all the techniques, to

get your dog used to performing around other dogs, and to pick up useful training tips.

The most important consideration when training a German Shepherd for Agility is to take it slowly, and not to attempt any piece of equipment before the dog is confident. German Shepherds are naturally cautious – particularly of new people and situations, so let your dog work at his own pace and do not rush him.

Keep training sessions short, but frequent, and do not forget to reward and/or praise your dog whenever he does well.

Teaching Commands

When teaching the pieces of equipment, you should use a command word so that your German Shepherd associates the word with the obstacle. Because speed is crucial in Agility, being able to direct your dog to the next piece of equipment while he is still on the first can shave off vital seconds from your course time. Below is a list of suggested words. If you choose your own, make sure they are short (so they can be said quickly) and that they sound different to the other commands used.

Tunnel	Through
Tyre	Tyre
Hurdle	Over
Long jump	Jump
Weaves	Weave
Dog walk	Walk
A-frame	Frame
See-saw	Saw
Pause table	Table

Body language is another important means of communicating with your dog, and is especially important with a breed like the German Shepherd that seems to have a natural skill at 'reading' his owner's body language and responding accordingly. You should always turn your body (particularly the shoulders) to the piece of equipment you would like your dog to tackle next.

Of course, there may be times when your dog is not able to see your body language, in which case you will have to rely solely on verbal commands.

The course designers are likely to do everything they can to trip your dog up with 'traps' – where your handling skills will be put to the utmost test. A trap is where a piece of equipment is laid immediately after another in such a way that, without proper direction, the dog may believe he is expected to tackle it. Tunnels and the contact pieces are often used as traps, as dogs enjoy them so much (their love of contacts comes from them being taught with so many treats).

The next step is to teach directional commands.

DIRECTION	COMMAND
For the dog to turn to his left	"Back"
For the dog to turn to his right	"Right"
For the dog to be on your left	"Heel"
For the dog to be on your right	"Rick"

Teaching your German Shepherd to turn left or right is simple if you link the word with the action.
- Throw a ball to your dog's left, tell him to fetch it, and as he turns left, say "Back".
- Repeat the procedure, this time throwing the ball to your dog's right, and giving the command "Right".
- Keep practising until your German Shepherd will turn left and right without the prompt of the ball.

Getting your dog on your left or right uses the same training principles. Traditionally, dogs ran on the left of the handler, but nowadays teaching is more relaxed and the dog is taught to be on whatever side the handler prefers, and according to what is quickest around the course.

For more information on training your dog to walk or run by your side, see page 73 on Obedience heel-work. A close heel is not required for Agility, but the exercises will get the dog used to coming to your side. Once he is happy on the left side, repeat the exercises with him on your right side, repeating the word 'rick'.

Tunnels

There are two types of tunnel that the dog is expected to run through – a rigid tunnel and a cloth tunnel that the dog has to push his way through. Tunnels are simple to teach, as long as you teach them in short sections.

- Shorten the tunnel (either by scrunching up

Start by training with a rigid, open tunnel.

Hurdles

An Agility course contains several hurdles. It can be dangerous to your German Shepherd's health if you teach the jumps at full height while he is still growing. The hurdles should be kept very low until he is fully matured physically.

- Put a broom handle on the floor, sit the other side of it, and encourage the dog to come to you.
- As soon as he goes over the broom, say "Over", or whatever command word you choose, and give him lots of fuss and praise.
- Gradually increase the height of the broom handle.
- If, when the height increases, your German Shepherd starts running under or around the jumps, rather than over them, put a long

the rigid tunnel or by folding back the material of the collapsible cloth tunnel). There should be very little distance between the entrance and exit – the dog should be able simply to step through it.

- Sit by the tunnel exit, and encourage the dog to come to you.
- As he steps forward, say "Tunnel", and reward and praise him when he reaches you.
- Every time he does it without fault, unscrunch (or fold down) a little more of the tunnel, so that your German Shepherd has a little further to come through, until eventually he can run through the entire tunnel.

Because some dogs find it unnerving to push their way through the collapsible tunnel, it is advisable to start with the rigid, open tunnel to build up your dog's confidence.

Keep the hurdle height low so your Shepherd is not tempted to duck underneath.

training lead on him, stand the other side of the jump (holding the lead) and encourage him over. Alternatively, place obstacles around and under the jump so that he has no option but to go over.

Long Jump/Broad Jump

The long jump is made up of several sections which make a gradual incline.

- Sit your German Shepherd in front of just one section.
- Stand the other side of the jump and encourage him over.
- As he leaps, say your command word (e.g. "Long").
- Reward him with praise and a treat (food or toy) every time he completes a jump successfully.
- Gradually add sections of the long jump until he can clear it all (remember to give a longer run-up, as you add more sections).

Tyre

The tyre can be a little trickier, as the jumping has to be more accurate, but thorough training should ensure there are few problems.

- Sit your German Shepherd one side of the tyre and you sit the other side.
- Hold your dog's favourite treat or toy right by the tyre and tempt him through it.
- If he insists on running around or under the tyre, put a training lead on him, put it through the tyre, and hold the other end.

With practice, your Shepherd will tackle the obstacle on command alone.

- When he leaps through the tyre, say your command word (e.g. "Tyre"), and give lots of praise and a reward.
- Keep practising, until eventually you no longer have to be the other side of the tyre, and you can instruct him through by the command word alone.

Weave

This obstacle consists of a number of poles which the dog is expected to 'weave' through. These look the simplest part of the course, but weaving accurately and at speed is generally recognised to be one of the most difficult exercises in Agility.

- Starting with the poles in their original position (one long line), move the first to the left, the second to the right, the third to the

Speed and accuracy are needed with the weaving poles.

left and so on, until you end up with two lines about a metre (three feet) apart, and parallel to each other.

- With a treat or toy in your hand, guide your German Shepherd through the central passage between the two lines. Say "Weave" as you do it, and praise and reward him when you get to the end.

- Move the poles in a little, and repeat.

- As the poles get closer to each other, your German Shepherd will no longer be able to walk in a straight line between the two lines, and will have to move between them. Bend forward and guide your dog through the poles, using a treat to encourage him through.

- As before, give lots of praise and give a treat (or play a quick game) when you get to the end.

- Keep moving the poles closer, until eventually they are back in their original position.

- Keep practising (in short but frequent sessions) to build up your speed. The key is to build up a rhythm so that your Shepherd 'bounces' through them.

Contact Equipment

The contact equipment is so called because your dog has to touch a marked area on the beginning and end of each piece of equipment. The areas exist not only to test the dog's accuracy, but also to protect the dog's safety, as leaping prematurely from the dog walk, see-saw or A-frame could cause injury. An obstacle is not considered complete unless contact is made on the marked areas.

You should initially teach your German Shepherd to stop on each marked contact point, so that, when he speeds up, it is instilled in him at least to slow down a little on the contact points and be sure to touch them. Walk your dog on to the point and stop when he is on it. Praise, pause, give a treat and then move on.

Dog Walk

The dog walk is a narrow walkway raised off the ground which has a slope at the front and end, each with a contact point. It is fairly simple to master, but training should not be rushed – methodical progress is better in the long term, and speed can then be worked on once the dog is confident and well practised.

- With your German Shepherd on a lead, walk him up to the start of the dog walk, and stop him when he is on the first contact.

The dog walk presents few problems – work at building up confidence rather than speed to begin with.

- Praise, pause, treat and move on, saying your command word (e.g. "Walk").
- Walking alongside him on the ground, walk him across the obstacle slowly, encouraging him the entire way.
- When you get to the end contact point, repeat as for the first.
- Give lots of praise and a reward when your dog has completed the piece.
- With practice, gradually build up the speed, always careful that contact is made with the marked points.

A-Frame

The A-frame is an A-shaped ramp which the dog should scale and descend. It is quite steep, so should not be attempted at full height until your German Shepherd is fully grown and his body can cope with the physical exertion. Until

that time, teach it flat on the ground, or slightly raised.

- Lay the A-frame completely flat on the ground.
- Walk your dog on to the first contact point, stop and reward, as for the other pieces of contact equipment.
- Walk on, saying your command word (e.g. "Frame") and repeat the contact procedure when you reach the last point.
- Practise a few times, before slightly raising the A-frame. Repeat as before.
- Keep increasing the frame's incline until it is at full height, remembering that, the steeper the incline, the longer the approach your Shepherd will need to run up it.

See-Saw

The see-saw can be tricky if you do not take training very slowly and carefully. Having the equipment move under his feet can be intimidating for the dog, especially for a German Shepherd who is notoriously suspicious and uneasy of new situations.

Stage one:
- Walk your German Shepherd on to the see-saw. Stop when he is on the first contact point, praise, pause, and move on.
- Walk him slowly up to the pivot point, saying "See-saw" (or "Saw" – as it is quicker to say).
- Give lots of reassurance, to encourage him to stay on the piece, so that he does not attempt to jump off.

- Keep practising getting him to the pivot point. When he is happy and confident on the piece, progress to stage two.

Stage two:
- When he is on the pivot point, encourage him to take a step forward, down the see-saw. Hold a treat or squeaky toy a short distance in front of him to tempt him forward.
- Praise and reassure him the whole time.
- Over the course of several training sessions, gradually extend the distance he will walk down the see-saw. Reward him with every step initially to build up his confidence.
- You can then progress to training your dog to walk up the see-saw, negotiating the pivot

The tilt of the seesaw can be quite alarming to begin with, so take it steady, and give lots of praise.

point and then down the other side (making contact with the final point).
- With practice, slowly build up his confidence and speed. Always accompany him until you are sure he is fully confident and has mastered the equipment (if something goes wrong, and he loses his nerve, it will take considerable remedial work to get him back on it).
- Give lots and lots of praise and affection when he completes the piece.

Pause Table

The dog has to jump on to a table and stay for a count of five. The judge may ask the dog to sit or to go down for the stay.

- Starting with a low table, use encouragement or a treat/toy to persuade your dog to jump on to the table.
- Once on, tell him to "Wait", and give him a treat or two until you have counted to five.
- Tell him to "Go" at the end of the wait, step back and encourage him to you, so he jumps off the table.
- Gradually prolong the length of time he is on the table before getting a treat, so that eventually you can withdraw the treats altogether.
- Once he gets the hang of what is expected, practise down-stays and sit-stays for the count of five.
- Remember to make your German Shepherd feel very clever every time he has completed the equipment.

THE MAX FACTOR

Nick Samuel finds Agility-training his German Shepherd, five-year-old Max, an incredibly rewarding experience.

"Max loves it," says Nick. "He is made for Agility. He's very food-oriented, which helps, and has a true working mentality – he likes to do a job, and is always ready to please and to show off. He's very intelligent. You only have to show him something once or twice and he's got it.

"When we queue up, waiting for our practice training run, he can hardly contain himself, and you can see him winding himself up.

"You have to be very careful with Shepherds not to damage their hips, and you should wait until the dog is at least a year old before starting any serious training. Before this time, you should do only very gentle exercises – and certainly no jumps.

"German Shepherds love being with their

Max has boundless enthusiasm for his Agility training.

owners, and Max is no exception. He doesn't need a vast amount of motivation at all. He is utterly focused when training with me, and is hardly ever distracted. He just wants to get in there and get the job done."

FLYBALL

Flyball is best described as a canine relay race. Two teams compete against each other on two identical tracks, each 51 feet long (15.5 metres). Each dog must leap the four hurdles, trigger a box to release a ball which the dog must catch, and then return to the starting-finishing line before the next dog can start.

If a ball is dropped, or a hurdle is knocked, it is deemed a fault, and the culprit must run the course again after the last member of the team has run. The team that completes in the fastest time wins.

Flyball is incredibly popular in the United States and the United Kingdom. It is fairly simple to teach, but is more difficult to be very good at, as the standard of the top teams is very high – America, Canada and the United Kingdom have all achieved team-times under 17 seconds.

Because of his size, the German Shepherd is not as naturally agile as, for example, the Border Collie or Working Collie. The Shepherd is a dedicated worker, and many have overcome their slight physical disadvantage, working that little bit harder, to compete in teams around the world.

HAVING A BALL

Until recently, Kay Burrow had always trained Border Collies (she currently has two: Mac and Cae). Her husband had always wanted a German Shepherd, so they bought Tia, and have since bought a Spanish Water Dog called Bramble. Kay has started training Tia for Flyball, a sport which she has taken to like a Spanish Water Dog to water!

"I don't think Tia is very typical of the breed," says Kay. "She is incredibly calm! After training Border Collies, who can be hyperactive and very headstrong, it's been much easier to work with Tia.

"We had a go at Agility, and my son does Obedience with her, but it's Flyball that she really enjoys – she just seems to have taken to it. It took no time at all to teach. She sat and watched us training the others. I took the box home to practise with my Spanish Water Dog, Bramble, and Tia just got up and decided to give it a go herself. She went up to the box, triggered the ball, and caught it!

"We have since introduced the jumps. We still have netting around the jumps, to make sure they jump *over* them rather than *around* them, but the netting will be removed soon, and then we can work on speeding them up and introducing them to a team.

"Tia can be fast when she wants to be. Sometimes she can be a little slow returning to me, but I just run away, and she speeds up to catch me. She is always accurate and conscientious, and, if she drops a ball, she won't come back until she's gone back to pick it up.

"Motivation is the key to having a successful Flyball competitor. Sometimes Tia works for a food treat, other times, all the reward she wants is a "Good Girl!". Whatever rewards are used, Tia loves Flyball which is the most important thing."

TIA IN ACTION

COMPETITIVE OBEDIENCE

The German Shepherd is an eager pupil in most canine sports, but especially so in competitive Obedience. The loyal Shepherd is born to serve, and will relish the opportunity to prove his dedication and intelligence, and, most of all, to please his owner.

This is not to say that training a German Shepherd is easy work – far from it. They need to be handled very sensitively to get the best out of them, and will not respond well to lengthy and monotonous training sessions. The key to having a successful Obedience Shepherd who enjoys working for you, is to make training fun. Frequent short sessions and lots of rewards will soon persuade your German Shepherd to enjoy himself.

Heelwork

German Shepherds are perfectionists. They are larger and less agile than Collies so have to work harder, but that is not to say that the same high standards cannot be achieved with practice.

Your dog is required to walk beside you on your left side, both on and off the lead, and to remain close (neither forward nor behind, but with his head level with your knee) whatever direction you take.

Attention and position are the basis of good heelwork.

- To get your German Shepherd used to the correct position from the very start, practise it standing still. Stand him on your left side, and hold a treat or toy in your right hand. Say "Watch".
- As he grows, you can move your right hand up, until eventually it is by your face, so that he learns to look at you (and this will make it easier should you dispense with the treat later).
- Practise standing for longer periods before even attempting to take a step forward, so that the correct position becomes second nature to your dog.
- Take a few steps forward, encouraging him forward with a treat. If he gets out of

---

ANGLO-AMERICAN DIFFERENCES

There are some variations between Obedience exercises performed in the UK and in the US. A closer, tighter position is required in UK heelwork, for example.

However, the same skills are tested (heelwork, scenting, retrieves and stays); it is just the detail which varies.

position, stop and put him in position, and start again.

- When he is in the right position, give lots of praise and a treat to keep him interested, and say your command word (e.g. "Watch" or "Heel").
- Practise walking at different speeds, so your German Shepherd learns to concentrate on staying in the right position.

Changing Direction

Once your German Shepherd can walk in the correct position even if you change your walking speed, it is time to introduce changes in direction.

- Get your German Shepherd in position by your side, and start off, as before, at a moderate pace.
- After a while walk in a large circle, anticlockwise. With your dog on your left side looking at your right hand, and with you gently curving left, you will be able to guide him into walking beside you.
- Keep practising, making the turns more pronounced. Then practise the same exercise, this time circling clockwise.

Send Away

This is where the dog is sent in a direction indicated by the judge, drops down at the owner's command, and is recalled in a certain direction (again, indicated by the judge).

Shepherds are renowned for being their owners' shadows, so the Send Away can be one of the harder Obedience exercises to master.

This is an advanced exercise, so do not despair if you can't master it straightaway.

Going

- Place a mat, or towel on the floor, and call your Shepherd to it, saying "Away".
- Praise and reward him when he goes to the mat. It is crucial that your dog sees going away on command as a positive, not a negative, experience.
- It may help if you place a treat on the mat to encourage the dog to it (though you must phase this out gradually or the dog will look for a treat when competing!).
- Practise the exercise, gradually increasing the distance you are from the mat.

Returning

When the dog is used to the first half of the exercise, practise the second part, where you must call the dog to heel while walking in a direction indicated by the judge. You must continue walking until asked to stop by the judge.

- See page 30 for recall training. To fine-tune the response, reward only the fastest responses, so your dog has to work harder to get the treat.
- Then practise recalling him while you are walking in a variety of directions, and instruct him to "Heel" (see above).
- Don't forget to praise and treat to show your dog when he has done something you approve of.

QUEEN OF SHEBA

Laurie Phillips has been involved in Competitive Obedience for many years. He has worked one Border Collie, but the rest of his dogs have been German Shepherds.

"I didn't start training Sheba, my most successful bitch, until she was two. Before that, I trained her to be an obedient dog, but not an Obedience dog. There is a difference.

"Motivating a German Shepherd is not difficult – you just have to find what works best for each dog. With some, it's food; others prefer toys. I had one dog that just wanted verbal praise, but I had to be careful to give her just the right amount. I had to give her enough to keep her focused, but too much would make her go all silly and giddy.

"The most important piece of advice for German Shepherd owners thinking of taking up Obedience is: join a club, though you must find one that uses kind training methods. Joining a club is important, as it is very easy to teach something in the wrong way, and then you have to live with the mistakes for the rest of the dog's career. I made the mistake with Sheba when teaching distance control. This is an exercise where the dog has to respond to commands, at a distance, but without moving more than a body's length in any direction.

"I was told that, initially, it was important to get the dog to respond to commands and not to worry about the moving forward – that you could deal with that once you have mastered obedience at a distance. But it is very difficult for the dog to unlearn something. It

is far better to teach it in the correct way from the very start. I struggled with Sheba's distance control throughout her Obedience career.

"Now, I teach it very differently. Because you must teach the pup to Sit, go Down and Stand, without the dog gaining any ground, I start with a 10-week-old pup on a grooming table. When grooming, I put the pup in the Sit, Down and Stand positions that are required for distance control, while saying the commands, and while ensuring the dog doesn't move forward during the exercise. Of course, the dog doesn't know what is happening, but it helps him get used to the positions and the command words.

"Another way is to teach the commands with the dog close by, and with an obstacle in front of him, so that he can't go forward. Then he will adjust how he goes down etc. When it is second-nature, then you can remove the obstacle.

"Another tip for the novice is to keep training fun. You see many German Shepherds in the lower classes, where people have started Obedience, but then numbers dwindle in the higher classes. This is usually because the owners overdo it and bore the pants off the dog. You must always do just enough to maintain his interest, and then stop. Ten minutes a day is much better than six days of nothing, and then 90 minutes in one go.

"Succeeding with a German Shepherd is a challenge, but it is very rewarding. There is nothing better than to see a Shepherd work. It fills me with pure joy to see one move around the ring."

FREESTYLE

Canine Freestyle, or Heelwork to Music, is becoming increasingly popular as a dog sport. Its foundations are in Obedience, but it goes beyond that to include various steps and moves where the handler and dog 'dance' together in time to the music, walking, turning, spinning and jumping to a chosen piece of music for a set period of time. It's great fun and good exercise, for both dog and handler, and, as you will discover, German Shepherds make great dancing partners. It is difficult to understand why there aren't many more Shepherd competitors. Big

SHYANN IN THE SPOTLIGHT

Nancy Malone from Houston, Texas, has a three-year-old German Shepherd Dog called ShyAnn, and has been doing Musical Freestyle with her for about two years. ShyAnn has an impressive background – she is currently rated as the number three German Shepherd in AKC Novice Agility. She has won more than 17 titles in Agility in less than nine months. With an obvious talent for being agile and accurate, Nancy decided to train ShyAnn for Freestyle. "I didn't know anything about Freestyle until about two years ago when our dog training club arranged for Carolyn Scott, from the Footloose Canine Freestyle Association, to do a two-day workshop on Freestyle. Carolyn came up and did the workshop, and I fell in love with the sport. I had always loved music and now I had the ability to combine the two things I loved: music and working with my German Shepherd Dog.

"It was much easier training Freestyle because ShyAnn had a good grasp of the basic Obedience commands, such as the 'go to heel' position, heeling, staying, etc. This meant she was ready to compete in just three months.

"Without a lot of practice and without knowing a lot about the sport, we entered our first competition in Houston in the Novice on-leash class. We danced to a song called *Apache* and we were both dressed up like Indians. We won first place and $200!

"Our routines don't always go without a hitch. One time, I was meant to skip backwards with ShyAnn coming forward directly in front of me. As I was skipping backwards, ShyAnn was supposed to catch up with me and then go through my legs, turn around and face me, and then stick out her foot to touch my foot. Instead, she went through and turned, but when I stuck out my foot, she took it in her mouth and held it! The crowd thought it was part of the routine and just cracked up with laughter.

Nancy with ShyAnn – partners in Canine Freestyle.

they may be, but clumsy they are not. A well-trained Shepherd, with the right music and handler, is graceful and agile – a joy to watch.

The sport is very popular in the United States, where the performances tend to be more elaborate and flamboyant, although this trend is beginning to be seen in the United Kingdom.

The competition rules vary according to the organisation putting on the show, but generally performances are under five minutes. Judging not only assesses the performance (accuracy, synchronisation and the degree of difficulty), but also the presentation (artistic flair and costume).

Of course, I was about to die. It was funny when I went back and looked at the video later.

"We are now working on a new number to the tune of *You are my Angel* and we are both going to be dressed up like angels. I am doing this song totally as a dedication to ShyAnn because I truly feel she was God's special gift to me. We have a bond that few people can understand."

"If you are a creative person, which I am, Freestyle allows you the opportunity to develop a routine completely on your own. Certain organisations have guidelines to follow which makes it easier to decide what types of moves you want to create. You are judged in two areas – Technical and Artistic, much like figure-skating. What your dog lacks in the technical area can be more than

ShyAnn shows a real liking for the sport.

made up in the artistic area, and *vice versa*.

"You can plan moves that work best with your particular dog. It also allows you to show off your dog's personality and charm, and allows for you to be creative in your costume design. Determining how to dress to portray the music is a big part of the fun.

"I think Freestyle also creates or tightens the bond that you have with your dog because you really must move as a team. I would highly recommend this sport to others. It is not very physically demanding, so most people can participate; nor is it breed-specific, so you can compete with almost any breed – although weaving through the legs with a Great Dane might be a little tough! Above all, the dogs seem to enjoy it."

WORKING TRIALS/TRACKING

In the United Kingdom, Working Trials involves Tracking, Agility and Obedience. It tests the dog's accuracy, concentration, temperament and strength, and is enjoyed by many healthy German Shepherds.

In the United States, many of the Working Trials skills are tested in competitive Obedience (e.g. heeling on and off lead, sit and down exercises, retrieving a dumb-bell over a solid high jump, broad jump over a series of low wooden hurdles etc.). For this reason, the Working Trials titles of Companion Dog, Companion Dog Excellent, and Utility Dog are also used in US Obedience (with the addition of Obedience Trials Champion – OTCh.). In the United States, the tracking element of Working Trials is a separate sport and has its own titles (see below).

Working Trial Titles

In Working Trials, there are several different levels, each one testing the handler's control, and the dog's agility and nosework. The levels get progressively more difficult. For example, the Companion Dog (CD) Stake involves:

- Heeling on and off leash
- Recall to handler
- Sending the dog away
- Two-minute Sit
- 10-minute Down
- Clear jump
- Long jump

Advanced training comes into play with exercises such as retrieving a dumbell over an obstacle.

- Scale, Stay, Recall
- Retrieve a dumb-bell
- Elementary search.

In US Obedience many of these skills are tested in both CD and CDX.

By the time you have passed Companion Dog, worked through Utility Dog (UD), Working Dog (WD) and Tracking Dog, you come to the ultimate test, Patrol Dog (PD), which not only tests the dog's advanced control, agility and nosework, but also involves a category on searching for criminals:

- Quartering the ground
- Test of courage
- Search and escort
- Recall from criminal
- Pursuit and detention of criminal.

To achieve such a high level of control, you must attend a Working Trials club for specialist training.

US Tracking Titles

The three tracking titles each test the dog's ability to identify and follow a human scent. These skills are used every day by life-saving rescue dogs all over the world.

Tracking Dogs (TD)

To earn his TD, a dog needs to follow a recent track (laid thirty minutes to two hours previously). The track of 440-500 yards will involve three to five turns (i.e. abrupt changes in direction), both to the left and to the right. The dog is also expected to retrieve or indicate the location of an article (glove or wallet).

Tracking Dog Excellent (TDX)

A TDX involves following an older track (laid three to five hours previously). The track is longer (800-1000 yards), more turns are involved (five to seven), and more demanding physical and scenting obstacles have to be overcome (such as cross-tracks). The dog should retrieve or indicate four different articles, all approximately the same size.

Variable Surface Tracking (VST)

This is the urban equivalent to the more traditional tracking titles, which are based in countryside surroundings. To earn his VST a dog must follow a 600- to 800-yard track laid three to five hours previously. It may take him down a street, through a building, and through other typical urban areas. The dog's ability to

A good tracking dog needs to use initiative as well as a good sense of smell.

ON THE RIGHT TRACK

Tony Fox is a very successful Obedience and Working Trials competitor and trainer. For him, tracking is an essential part of a trial, and tests the teamwork of dog and handler to the full.

"The exhilaration is the greatest feeling," he says. "When you reach the end of a long, difficult track, the sense of relief and achievement is wonderful. It's a lonely place out there – you are out in the middle of nowhere, watching your dog sniffing about, and you are wondering if he is following the right scent and if the judge is about to intervene and fail you.

"Sometimes your dog will lead you to a dead rabbit, and you realise he's been following the wrong scent. Whenever you are out walking, you have to discourage your dog from sniffing carcases and droppings so that he does not stray from the right scent when tracking in a competition.

"The key to tracking successfully is to read your dog and learn how to handle the line. Once friends put me in a harness on a moor to show me how it felt for the dog! They were very experienced and I could feel them steering me left and right. How you handle the line definitely influences the dog.

"One tip is that if you suspect you are reaching a turn, shorten up the lead

and see how your dog reacts. If he is sure of the right track, he will insist on pulling ahead; if he is a little uncertain, he won't pull – and then won't wander aimlessly following the wrong track.

"You should talk to your dog and remain alert. There may be times when your dog might be struggling, but you may notice a footprint. Though there's no guarantee it will be the right track, it could be a clue.

"Tracking can be so different depending on where the competition is (what part of the country and hence what type of ground), the seasons (whether it is dry, hard ground, or long, wet grass), and the weather (it could be glorious sunshine, rain, or snow). Each have their different challenges."

Blueboy Of Foxfold CDex, UDex, WDex, owned and trained by Tony Fox.

track on different surfaces is also tested (vegetation, concrete, asphalt, gravel, sand etc.). Four to eight turns are involved, and four items should be found.

Teaching Searching

For a taster of basic tracking, try the following with your dog or pup. German Shepherds have an excellent nose, and love to use it, and your Shepherd should find it an enjoyable game.

- You can start the basics of tracking with a young pup. Take his favourite toy, and, with him watching you, put it behind a cushion. Then ask the pup: "Where's your ball? Go find!". As soon as he finds it, heap lots of praise on him and have a game with the ball/toy.
- Gradually progress to hiding it without the pup seeing where you have put it. Keep the search within a fairly small area at first, so he never has to look too far. Each time, praise and reward him for finding it.
- Do not let the pup have too much access to the toy – it has to remain 'special' or he won't be that bothered to look for it.

When he is about six or seven months you can progress to taking his toy and throwing it a little way in a field of fairly long grass. Tell him to "Go find!". Your dog will know it is there, but won't be able to see it, so will have to search for it. It is very important that he learns not to rely always on his eyes – rather, on his nose. With practice, you can increase the area he has to search.

Teaching Tracking

Tracking, where the dog follows a scent-trail, follows the same principle.

- Take the dog's blanket, or an old jumper of yours (with your scent on), and make a very short trail in long grass.
- Take the dog to the area, and tell him to "Go find!".
- When he does, give lots and lots of praise and a reward. If he doesn't find it, walk nearer to it, until he does, and then make him feel very clever.
- Gradually progress to longer tracks, using smaller objects. Slowly introduce turns (starting with gradual curves and making them more pronounced).

Your dog should eventually learn to follow the track of footsteps, rather than the trail of a dragged item.

- Put your dog in a sit-stay. Walk a short distance in front of him, put his favourite toy down and tell him to "Go find!". Praise when he finds his toy.
- Gradually increase the difficulty – increasing the distance you walk, introducing curves etc, until he is able to follow a complicated track.
- When he is well practised, walk and hide his toy out of sight and see if he can pick up the track.
- Once he has mastered this, make the scent less obvious by leaving it for longer periods of time before the dog is let loose on it.

HERDING

Until the American Kennel Club Herding Tests and Trial programme was developed more than a decade ago, many people were not aware of the German Shepherd's herding past – despite the breed's name! The AKC tests and trials, which preserve and showcase the instinctive herding skills inherent in the breed, are grouped into two beginning levels: the Herding Test (HT) and Pre-trial Test (PT) in which the dog must show controlled movement of the stock (either sheep, cows or ducks). There are also three advanced trial courses:

• Course A demonstrates the versatility of an all-round ranch or farm dog.
• Course B requires the dog to show an ability to control and move stock in a very large, open field.
• Course C (sheep only) requires the dog to 'tend' to the sheep – to accompany the flock from their pen, up roads and over bridges, to various grazing areas for the day, and then return safely home with the flock.

German Shepherd Dogs are versatile enough to perform all the courses, but the A and C are the most popular. In the C course, the dog's 'flying trot', typical of the breed, may be observed as the dogs serve as 'living fences' in maintaining a large group of sheep in a small grazing area. Since these trials are 'simulations' of real situations, the numbers of sheep are minimal (three to five) for both the A and B Courses, and 20 or more sheep for the C Course.

NATURAL TALENT

Dorothy Linn from Belmont, California, has been herding for seven years, and has been Show Chairman of four of the German Shepherd Dog Club of America's National Specialty Herding events. She still remembers the difficulties of her early training days.

"I started training Tigger, my first dog and a breed Champion, when I was invited to bring him for an instinct test offered by a leading instructor, exhibitor and judge. Tigger immediately started gathering and driving the sheep towards the instructor, even though he had never seen a sheep in his life. I was so fascinated with what this dog demonstrated that I was encouraged to step in myself to try to learn to handle and work with my own dog.

"The instinct tests are very important and show if a dog has sufficient promise to continue on to competition levels. Herding is actually a controlled prey drive, and the instinct tests show to what degree this is inherently present in each dog. Some dogs have a lot more prey drive than others. However, it is rare to see a German Shepherd Dog so obsessed with the desire to kill sheep that they cannot be controlled. If this happens, they are quickly removed from any chance of ever seeing sheep again.

"Dogs with a strong prey drive get pretty excited and one thinks they will 'eat sheep', but they can actually become the best herding dogs because, once taught to back off and to control themselves, they have great focus and concentration on the livestock.

"You may feel easier working with a dog with less prey drive, but it takes just one pause to sniff the daisies or pose for the exhibitors (I had a Champion that loved to do this!), and those smart sheep will sprint like rabbits for home – all in different directions. Then the dog has to start all over again trying to gather them in a flock, wasting precious time.

"A dog with no prey drive at all – well, that's just a lost cause, as you end up walking with a bunch of sheep and no dog!

"After some training, I tried Tigger at the 1993 National Trial. I entered him in the beginner's level – HT – and I was very much a novice owner. Tigger was immensely talented, and prior to the test, I was still having difficulty (stumbling over heavy, woolly sheep) moving fast enough for my dog. If he thought I was too slow, he would grip a chunk of wool on a sheep leg to try to hurry them up. This is absolutely forbidden, a sure failure to qualify in competition.

"The traditional staff was too heavy for me, so I was using a bamboo garden stake to slap on the ground to get his attention to back off the sheep. For good luck, a friend presented me with a fresh green bamboo pole just cut from her garden, before I entered the ring.

"Before we went in, I showed the pole to Tigger and told him he had better behave in the ring. He gave me a good, hard look, and went

Tigger taking control in Herding Trials.

through his two tests, under two different judges, with two first-ever perfect 'no-grip' runs.

"Since this made him a dual Champion, I was ecstatic. Then the judges lectured me that this dog was much smarter than his owner, and that he should be trusted much more! But then, everyone that has a German Shepherd knows that they are smarter than the average human!

"Tigger has since passed on – he was one of my favourite dogs because of the bond we developed when working together. I am now working other Shepherds, and I cannot describe the joy in watching my dogs happily and instinctively perform the job they were originally bred to do."

The herding instinct in the German Shepherd has survived intact.

SHOWING

A good German Shepherd showing and moving well is a joy to watch – the breed's size and charisma means he has a great presence in the ring. Well-trained dogs and experienced handlers make the whole process look easy, but considerable expertise and hard work goes into producing such professional results.

This is not to say that showing is an area inaccessible to the novice. There are many people at ring-training classes and in breed clubs who are more than willing to share their experience and to take a willing novice under their wing. With time, commitment, a good dog, and a little advice from experienced exhibitors, the show world is your oyster.

Don't be disheartened if success does not come at once. You will get better as your confidence and handling skills improve. Ask the advice of some experienced competitors who may give you some tips, or who may even advise you not to continue with your current dog. However, even with a good dog and competent handling skills, it is still very difficult to be successful because of the sheer numbers of excellent competitors in the German Shepherd class.

Preparation

At ring-training you will learn to present your dog correctly. You will learn the correct stance and how to achieve it; how best to show your dog's movement when running in the ring; and your dog will become familiar with being examined by a judge, and with being well behaved when surrounded by many other dogs.

These classes are excellent preparation for your first class, and will give you and your dog confidence and experience in a similar ring environment.

Your First Show

When you feel you and your dog are ready, check the dog press for details of forthcoming shows, and send off for schedules of those that you are interested in. Open or Specialty shows are good first shows as they will give you the experience of competing against other German Shepherds.

When you get in the ring, the judge may ask

The breeder will help you to assess a puppy to see if it has show potential.

all the competitors to run around the ring so that he or she can assess the overall quality of the class. It also helps to calm the dogs.

The judge will then assess the dogs individually, and may ask you to move your dog in a triangle or up and down in a straight line, so that his movement can be assessed. Movement is a very important feature of the German Shepherd. Because of his shepherding background, he should retain his 'trotting' qualities, and the ability to cover as much ground with as little effort as possible. His strides should be long and powerful, and his topline should remain fairly level (see Chapter Seven).

The judge will assess the overall appearance of your dog, and will then compare his structure against that of the ideal as laid out in the Standard. As well as checking the teeth, he or she will also feel for the correct skeletal structure and angulation.

Creating Champions

In the UK, the German Shepherd is in the Pastoral Group. There are a variety of different types of show, including Limited, Open and Championship.

- **Limited** shows can only be entered by members of the organisation putting on the show. The majority of classes will be 'any variety' classes where different breeds within the same Group compete against each other.
- **Open**, as its name suggests, is open to anyone. It will have breed classes as well as 'any variety' classes.

Not only must you have an excellent specimen of the breed, you must also learn the art of showing your Shepherd.

- **Championship** shows are bigger as there is more at stake. For each breed, there are two sets of Challenge Certificates or 'tickets' – one for the best bitch and one for the best dog. At the end of all the breed classes, the winners will go into a final class to compete for the ticket. Any dog or bitch that wins three tickets under three different judges becomes a Show Champion.

In the United States, the German Shepherd is in the Herding Group. Competitors can take part in two types of show: 'licensed', or 'point', shows (where Championship points are on offer), and 'informal', or 'match', shows (where no points are awarded). There are two types of licensed show:

- **Specialty** where dogs of a designated breed or grouping of breeds can compete against each other.
- **All-breed** where competitors can compete in scheduled classes for all breeds. The breed winners are judged within their Groups, and the Group winners then compete for Best In Show.

A Champion is created when a dog wins 15 points under three different judges. The 15 points need to include two 'majors' (three-, four-, or five-point awards), awarded by separate judges.

PRESENTING POPPY

Sheila Bell has been showing for six years, and it has been a steep learning curve for both her and her Shepherds.

"I bought my first German Shepherd, Gemma, for showing, and started training her at home. When she was four months old, I started training her at home. Initially, I would put her in the Stand position and tell her to 'Stand'.

"Once she understood the command, I taught her to Stay. Finally, we worked on movement and turning, so that she would turn well with me in the ring. Starting young, she soon picked up what was expected of her. As soon as I knew she understood, I would move on so she wouldn't become bored.

"I also took her to ring-training classes. Although Gemma had learnt many of the commands at home, the classes were very important for her to socialise with other dogs, and to get used to having strangers handle her.

"The German Shepherd is meant to be cautious of strangers, so it is important to get them used to being stroked, patted and checked over by a variety of different people. The classes were also useful for me – I was able to meet other breeders and to see other dogs, and I soon realised Gemma looked different.

"By comparing her to bitches of the same age, I saw that Gemma looked different. Unfortunately, she ended up too tall for the Breed Standard – often being mistaken for a male dog. She had a wonderful nature, though.

"I spoke with a top breeder who took me under his wing, and taught me how to recognise a good dog. My mentor taught me that if you wish to succeed, your winning must begin at home. You must prove yourself by work, dedication, and love for the breed. You cannot learn everything overnight – experience is the only way.

"I then bought another bitch puppy, Poppy. I knew more about what I was doing this time round (both at selecting and showing) and she won Best Puppy at her first show.

"I was excited to have such a big win (for me) so early on, and it made me determined to carry on showing, and to get even better. As well as Poppy being a better show dog, I was more experienced in the ring – and confidence makes a lot of difference. Poppy went on to win numerous first places at Open and Championship shows.

"I have bred from Poppy now, and her daughters (Becky and Claire) are doing well in the ring, too. They both love showing. As soon as I pick up the show lead, they get really excited and can't get in the car quick enough. Not all dogs enjoy the travelling and showing, though. I knew one dog who liked the going out and travelling, but hated the showing part!

"Ultimately, it is all about the dog. Your dog has to enjoy it if you are going to do well."

Becky, a daughter of Poppy, is carrying on the winning line.

CHAPTER SIX

A SPECIAL BOND

The German Shepherd was bred to work, and although he is no longer extensively used to herd, watch over, and guard sheep, his 'work ethic' is still as strong as ever. Several organisations have found that, with the breed's high intelligence and love of pleasing his owner, his need to work can be channelled successfully not only into fighting crime, but also into assistance (service) dog work.

POLICE DOGS

As early as 1901 the Verein für Schäferhunde (SV) approached the German police force about using German Shepherds. The club saw how the breed's guarding instincts could be employed in the defence of police officers. Trials proved successful – especially when it was shown that German Shepherds excelled in nosework.

The breed's excellent tracking skills have served it well. The First World War saw

Shepherds being used to find wounded soldiers. Today they are still used as Search and Rescue Dogs, finding victims of earthquakes and avalanches.

It is as police dogs, however, that the breed is most renowned, as they are used extensively all over the world – and with good reason. German Shepherds form strong attachments to their owners, and are loyal to the last – essential skills when you are relying on your dog to protect your life.

German Shepherds excel as police dogs

THE LAW ENFORCERS

William McNaughton, a police officer from New York City, works as an assistant trainer at the canine unit. In his 14 years, he has had three German Shepherds, and would not work with any other breed.

"We use only German Shepherds, because they have a proven record as police dogs," he says. "They are good all-rounders, and, more importantly, they have the right disposition, as the dogs must be tough while at work, but then go home with their owner and be a family dog.

"It's like having two different dogs, though some dogs, like some police officers, I guess, find it hard to switch off when they get home. My second dog, Sam, was like that. He was totally a one-man dog, and wasn't close to my wife and three kids – he just tolerated them. My current dog, George, is very much a family dog off-duty, and would play ball with the kids until their arms fall off.

"George is aggressive during training for criminal apprehension only because he is told to be. He isn't doing it out of viciousness, so I don't have any problems with him living in the same house as my kids.

"I know George would defend me if I was in trouble. In criminal apprehension training, he is told to go and bite a guy (who is playing a 'baddie'), and he does as he is told. The guy then pushes or hits me, and you should see the difference between the bites. The difference in pressure after I have been attacked is phenomenal.

"All dogs here have 16 weeks of training, during which they must complete 540 hours. This involves tracking, obedience, agility, and criminal apprehension. An examiner from another police force comes and tests the dogs,

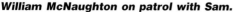
William McNaughton on patrol with Sam.

and continues to come once a month for the duration of the time the dog is in service.

"George has been in service for a year. Things have been quite quiet so far, but he did find a rape suspect hiding in a house, and was quick and effective in his response.

"Unfortunately, Sam had to be put down recently, because he had a bone tumour. He was fit and healthy till the end. I was out with him one day, and he yelped. Now, this is a dog that can take pain – he once broke his foot and still continued running – so I knew something was wrong. He was diagnosed with cancer, and three months

Working on a new partnership with George.

later, he was put to sleep. It was one of the toughest things I have ever had to do. He was a beautiful dog.

"The bond you have with your police dog is very close. I spend more time with my dog than I do my wife. I am with him 24 hours a day, seven days a week. George never leaves my side, he's there all the time. It can be overwhelming sometimes, and I put him in the yard to have a break. Then he whines at the door, wanting to be with me. So much for them being tough police dogs! They are just big babies – bottom line, that's what they are."

GUIDE DOGS

Most people's perception of a Guide Dog is of a Labrador or a Golden Retriever. However, the first Guide Dogs, back in the 1930s, were German Shepherds and it was a number of years before the Retriever breeds took over in popularity.

Although there are not so many Shepherds working as Guide Dogs, the breed is still highly valued in this work. In Britain, German Shepherds make up about 5 per cent of Guide

Dogs, and in the United States, Guide Dogs of America put the figure at 10 per cent.

Although they can be a little more temperamental than other breeds, German Shepherds are devoted to their masters and form strong attachments to them. They have a high level of concentration, and are willing and capable of a high workload. A good breeding programme and early, thorough, and on-going socialisation ensures that they don't become overprotective of their owners.

BONDING WITH BARCLAY

Lewis Pryce is a fund-raising manager at the Guide Dog centre in Cardiff. His Guide Dogs have included a Labrador and two German Shepherds. A Shepherd fan, who had the breed as a family pet when a child, Lewis requested that his second and third Guide Dogs be German Shepherds.

"I have always liked Shepherds," he says. "They are very intelligent, and they are superb working dogs – all my Shepherd Guide Dogs have lived up to all my expectations. They seem to be more alert and aware of other animals, people, and traffic than other breeds.

"My first Guide Dog, a Labrador, was undersize for the breed. She had large ears and looked very sweet. People couldn't help but come up to her. When I got Bury, my first German Shepherd, I thought 'Well, at least she won't attract so much attention,' but it was just the same, as people would come up and say, 'Oh, you don't see many Alsatians as Guide Dogs!' Barclay, my current German Shepherd, is a big dog, and gets even more attention!

"Barclay is an amazing dog, with a temperament that cannot be beaten. He is laid-back, has a thick, shaggy coat, and is adored wherever he goes. He loves cars. If you drive him anywhere, he will be your best friend, but he *respects* me.

"Shepherds are so keen to please, you don't have to be too firm with them. Bury was a very dominant bitch. When free in the park, she would go down like a sheepdog, and run and bowl other dogs over. If I simply raised my voice, her ears would go down and she would be very hurt. I have never had to raise my voice to Barclay, who is now aged seven.

"Because Shepherds become so attached to people, it can be difficult getting them to transfer their loyalty from the puppy socialiser and trainer to the owner. It took about 12 months for Barclay to bond fully with me, and even a couple of years later, whenever he saw his trainer, he would be over the moon – his back end would wiggle, and his tail would wag furiously.

"Shepherds should not be allowed to become overprotective of their owner, or territorial. Barclay comes to work with me, accompanies me to the pub, and to the city centre, so meets lots of different people. If the neighbours are having a day out on the beach, they sometimes take Barclay with them, too.

Lewis Pryce with Guide Dog Barclay.

"Shepherds have an amazing sense of direction, and can learn routes very quickly. Barclay is no exception. I once went to the bank on a Friday afternoon, and, because of the time, it wasn't worth going back to work. I went to the dry-cleaners, and was going to head home, but Barclay wanted to go a different route, so I let him. He went through streets that he's never been through before and ended up at our local pub!

"I can say with confidence that, with each of my Guide Dogs, I have been able to go anywhere in Cardiff with complete confidence. Although I was fond of my Labrador, for me, the Shepherd will always be superior. They are peaceful dogs, and make such very close companions."

THERAPY DOGS

Contact with pets is shown to be beneficial to our health and well-being. Many people – such as the elderly in many residential homes, or hospital or hospice patients – are unable to have a pet. For those who have been used to owning a dog, this can be devastating – and life can seem very empty and lonely indeed. Schemes where well-behaved dogs visit residents and patients in a range of different establishments are becoming increasingly popular in both the US and the UK, and German Shepherds have been found to make excellent therapy dogs.

SEFFE AND SOUND

Christine Phillips, a dog trainer from King's Lynn, Norfolk, has recently started visiting, with her German Shepherd Dog called Seffe.

"It's something I always wanted to do," says Christine, "but it was a case of having the time to do it. You can't go one week and not the next, it isn't fair. You have to commit to regular visits. Plus, you must have the right dog. All my Shepherds have good temperaments, but some are more suited to this type of work than others.

"Seffe is a nice-tempered bitch. She really loves people – she's very much a 'people dog' – and adores being made a fuss of. She's young (two years), but calm, and she seems to understand when people want to pat her. If you saw her in the garden now, you would think 'That dog's not calm!', but when visiting, she is very well behaved.

Seffe – a friend to both young and old.

"At the moment we are visiting a long-care hospital ward for the elderly. I wondered if the patients would be a bit apprehensive with such a big dog, but they love her. She sits by their side, leans against the wheelchairs, and looks up at them.

"We will soon start visiting a pre-school playgroup, which I have done with one of my other dogs in the past. It is so important that children have contact with dogs, as they are the next generation, and must be taught how to approach and respect dogs. Fortunately, children are so biddable and really listen to what is said.

"Several of the elderly have speech difficulties due to strokes or other illnesses, and they all respond to Seffe. I think they build an instant rapport with the dog because they can chat away to her and she responds to them. It seems to be a real communication breakthrough".

DOGS FOR THE DISABLED

A German Shepherd with the right temperament and a sound skeletal structure makes a great Dog for the Disabled, working at a consistently high level. The breed can be very sensitive, and so is particularly suited to owners that can give quiet, gentle handling. Once recipients have worked with a German Shepherd, they often say they won't work with any other breed.

This is a sentiment shared by Ann Greenwood from Bodmin, Cornwall. Suffering from a degenerative spine condition, Ann can walk a short distance, but relies mainly on a wheelchair to get around. German Shepherd Baron is Ann's second Dog for the Disabled. Her first, Shep, was a Border Collie, who has now retired, but who still lives with her.

"What does Baron do for me? In the morning, he puts the lights on, and collects my clothes for me to get dressed. He gets his lead for us to go to the horses, where he will collect the feed bins. He fetches anything I drop, gets me undressed at night, and turns me over in bed. He answers the phone, collects the milk, gets my money from the post office... everything really.

Baron is Ann Greenwood's second Dog for the Disabled.

"Because of my condition, bending down to pick things up is very difficult and can aggravate my condition, so Baron is a great help. The German Shepherd is very different to the Border Collie. If I was out with Shep and was busy doing something, he would go off and chase a pheasant or something. But Baron never moves from me. He is loose all the time, but is locked to me. He is very clever. He knows that if I ask him to turn the light off, and he lies there long enough, Shep will get up and do it for him!

"Shep knew about 100 commands. Baron was well on the way to learning them all within just three weeks of training. His size and strength is another asset. I have a 12-foot gate, and in gale-force winds Shep just didn't have the strength to close it – but Baron will never give in and is strong enough to cope with more physical demands. He also helps me to walk and is exactly the right height. He learned very quickly that when he is on my left-hand side he can walk

Baron performing his daily tasks – bringing in the milk, and helping with the washing.

at wheelchair pace, and if he is on my right-hand side in the harness, he must walk slowly, and wait to be told to take a pace.

"Baron is very eager to please. If I asked Shep to do something, he would wait until I finished the whole sentence, but Baron is gone on the "Fetch", without hearing *what* I want fetched! He'll come back with socks, shoes, anything... he's so keen, he can't understand why he should wait for all the instructions!

"He uses his initiative a lot. I have a donkey that likes to stand in his bowl when she's finished eating. Baron worked out that if he tugged hard enough, she would get out, and he could then bring the bowl to me. If I'm not ready to take the bowl, he'll take it into the food store. I never taught him that – he worked it out for himself.

"Baron was a trained guide dog, but he was retired early as he freaked one day in a heavy

traffic area. He lived with an elderly gentleman who left him alone quite a lot to visit his son and daughter, but Baron needs his owner with him all the time. If I leave him with my mother (who lives with us) for just a couple of hours to go out horse riding, he will wait by the patio doors, nose to the glass. Shep would just go off and amuse himself, but Baron isn't happy unless he is with me. He is definitely a one-man dog. He can't be left in kennels – he just freaks. Even his Guide Dog trainer used to have to take him home at night.

"Because of his guide dog training, we had to work on Baron's heelwork, as he was used to standing slightly in front of me, as if he was in a harness. In training, Baron will do something more for the joy of doing it than for the reward at the end. To him, working and training is just a big game."

CHAPTER SEVEN

SEEKING PERFECTION

The German Shepherd is different to all other breeds. What makes him look and behave so uniquely? Like all purebred dogs, a distinct set of qualities have been bred into him over many generations which differentiate him from every other breed – even those bred to do very similar jobs.

A German Shepherd is one of the world's most popular breeds. To make sure that he retains his original working ability and the physique to perform the job to the best of his ability, breeders use a Breed Standard. This is a written description of the ideal German Shepherd, detailing coat, conformation, colour and character. It is the blueprint for the breed which ensures that all the qualities which make the German Shepherd special will be retained.

There are wider implications as regards health and breeding programmes. As with all purebreds, inherited conditions do occur, and it is only by following the stipulations of the Breed Standard and researching into the bloodlines of all breeding stock that the future health and well-being of the German Shepherd can be guaranteed.

THE BREED STANDARD

The following analysis is a summary of the key points of the Breed Standards drawn up by the English and American Kennel Clubs. Contact your national kennel club for a copy of the Standard that specifically applies to you.

General Appearance/Characteristics
Alert, well-balanced, powerful and well-muscled, the German Shepherd's working ability should be immediately apparent. This ability is paramount and the dog's looks should never take precedence. The individual should give a clear impression of masculinity or femininity.

Temperament
A German Shepherd's temperament is his most

important quality. He should be courageous, confident and biddable, and *never* aggressive, nervous or shy.

Head And Skull

The head should be in proportion with the body. The forehead should have a slight curve, and should blend into the long, strong muzzle effortlessly.

Eyes

The medium-sized, almond-shaped eyes should not protrude, and should be as dark as possible, complementing the dark, rich coat. He should have an intelligent expression.

German Shepherds should give a distinct impression of masculinity (above) or femininity (below).

Ears

The German Shepherd's fairly pointed ears should be erect and face forward, so that even the faintest sounds will be picked up (such as a lost sheep, or a predator's approach). The centre lines of the ears should, ideally, be parallel to each other.

Mouth

The muzzle topline should be parallel to that of the skull. The jaws should be strong (originally, he would nip sheep in order to herd them into the desired direction) and the strong, healthy teeth should be arranged in a scissor-bite formation (the upper teeth closely overlapping the lower teeth). Without a scissor-bite, the dog will not be able to close its mouth properly, and so loses considerable strength and power, and may not be able to defend its wards from predators quite so ardently.

Neck

The neck should be muscular and fairly long (though still in proportion to the size of the head).

Forequarters

Forequarters are strong and well-muscled. Long shoulder-blades laid flat on the body at an approximate right angle. Forelegs are straight, and the pasterns are slightly angulated.

Body

The German Shepherd should be slightly longer than he is tall. He should have a deep chest with plenty of room for heart and lungs. The ribs should neither be flat nor barrel-shaped. The withers are high and join the topline, which slightly slopes from the top end of the dog to the bottom. The back should be straight.

Hindquarters

Strong, broad and well-muscled, to propel the body forward with the least effort. The short, straight, powerful hocks ensure the German Shepherd can turn quickly, an important skill when herding.

The forequarters are strong and well-muscled.

The hindquarters are broad, with short, powerful hocks.

Feet

The arched foot is a cross between a cat foot and hare foot. This is so that, in soft ground, the foot will spread out, and, together with the webbed feet, this ensures the dog has a wider surface area so that he doesn't sink in mud etc. The pads should be hard-wearing to protect against all kinds of terrain. The nails should be short and dark.

Tail

The bushy German Shepherd tail should hang slightly curved, like a sabre, and, ideally, should not be carried above the level of the back.

Gait/Movement

This is a very important aspect of the German Shepherd Dog. As a shepherd, he had to be able to cover a lot of ground, and so energy-efficient movement was vital. Because he is a trotting dog, he needs a long stride to cover the most ground with the least number of steps. Each foreleg moves simultaneously with the diagonally opposite hindleg. The hindquarters really thrust the body forward. The backline should remain fairly level.

Coat

The German Shepherd has a waterproof double coat to maintain warmth when out shepherding in hostile conditions. The outer coat should be straight, close-lying and as dense as possible. Hair on the head (and inner ear), and on the front of the legs and paws is shorter, while longer hair can be found on the neck and on the back of the legs.

Colour

The German Shepherd varies in colour. In the US, most rich colours are permissible. In the UK, the following colours are acceptable: black; black saddle with tan or gold to light grey markings; all black; and all grey with lighter or brown markings ('sables'). Both countries frown on pale colours, such as white, blue, liver, and albino.

Although white pet German Shepherds are very attractive and popular, the Breed Standard discourages the pale colours in pedigree dogs.

The classic black saddle with gold markings.

ABOVE: *Sable is a grey colour with lighter or brown markings.*

BELOW: *White Shepherds have an enthusiastic following, but they do not conform to the Breed Standard.*

This is because the Breed Standard aims to preserve the original working dog. Light colours are undesirable in a shepherding dog, as he would be difficult to spot in a snowy landscape. The German Shepherd would also need to be dark to remain inconspicuous at night when watching his wards.

Size

In the US, a male German Shepherd should be 24-26 inches (60-65cms) and a bitch 22-24 inches (55-60 cms). In the UK, these sizes are also permissible, though the middle point of each one is deemed ideal – i.e. 25 inches (62.5 cms) for dogs, and 23 inches (57.5 cms) for bitches.

UNDERSTANDING PEDIGREES

There are three different ways of achieving the ideal German Shepherd as laid out in the Breed Standard:

- in-breeding
- line-breeding
- out-crossing.

Each of the above relates to how closely the stud dog and the brood bitch are related. All three can produce sound, typical dogs, as long as the dogs in the pedigree are good, healthy examples of the breed with excellent temperaments. The three dogs used to illustrated each type of breeding are all Champions (see pages 104 -106).

PUPPY TO CHAMPION

Looking at a young pup, it can be difficult to see how he will turn out. No breeder can guarantee a promising pup will develop into a Champion. In his first year to 18 months, your German Shepherd will undergo many physical changes – and even the most experienced breeder cannot foresee the eventual result. But the waiting and anticipating is all part of the fun.

Below are a selection of photos of Ch. Ibbsparr Mr President, showing his development from pup to Champion.

However *your* German Shepherd develops, in your eyes he will always be the most beautiful, loyal dog in the world – and that's really all that matters.

Ch. Ibbsparr Mr President ('Brit')

Brit aged four months.

At eight months, the difference is spectacular.

A mature dog, Brit at 18 months.

Ch. Ibbsparr Mr President aged three years.

In-breeding

In-breeding involves the mating of two very closely related animals, and is used when the breeder wants to emphasise very quickly a particular trait associated with the family.

This type of programme is not for the novice – as well as accentuating strengths, it can also accentuate faults, so should not be used without considerable planning. It should be left to experienced breeders, with detailed knowledge of the dogs' histories.

Lornaville Vaguely Noble – tight family breeding.

Parents	Grandparents	Great-Grandparents	Great-Great-Grandparents
Champion Lornaville Mr Bee	Lornaville Ambassador	Ch. Tarquin Of Dawnway	Ch. Eclipse Of Eveley
			Masquerade Of Dawnway
		Balacents Nora Of Lornaville	Ch. Rossfort Oran Of Kenmil
			Almerine Of Balacents
	Lornaville War Lady	Domonic Of Dawnway	Ch. Spartacist Of Hendrawen
			Melody Of Dawnway
		Hargret Rivercroft Brynylon Of Lornaville	Ch. Hendrawen Syrious Norge
			Ch. Harget Rivercroft Nylon
Champion Lornaville Anastasia	Lornaville Ambassador	Ch. Tarquin Of Dawnway	Ch. Eclipse Of Everly
			Masquerade Of Dawnway
		Balacents Nora Of Lornaville	Ch. Rossfort Oran Of Kenmil
			Almerine Of Balacents
	Lornaville Her Ladyship	Ch. Spartacist Of Hendrawen	Ch. Ramacon Swashbuckler
			Flicka Of Brinton
		Lornaville Annabell	Ch. Tarquin Of Dawnway
			Balacents Nora Of Lornaville

Line-breeding

This also involves mating related dogs, but those that are not as closely linked. It is used to maintain or consolidate ('fix') the characteristics of the line, while still introducing some new blood. Of course, as well as 'fixing' the good points, you can also 'fix' the bad. Before deciding to line-breed, both parents should be assessed. If their good points outweigh their faults, then examine the parents' pedigrees to ensure the line is free of all congenital abnormalities and that the dogs are loyal, intelligent and courageous.

Penwartha Ice Man: an example of line-breeding.

Parents	Grandparents	Great-Grandparents	Great-Great-Grandparents
Ch. Velindre Viscount	King Of The Castle	Karashea-s Charlie Of Velindre	Ch. Eveleys Bonnie Prince Charlie
			Quowonder Quintessence
		Velindre Brocade	Velindre Jaeger
			Velindre Cass
	Ravenways Justine At Velindre	Ch. Kerson Kyerk	Ch. Amulrees Heiko
			Eumore Delight Of Kerson
		Ch. Karashea-s Amorous	Ch. Manven Oriel Of Ravenways
			Quowonder Quintessence
Midnight Maiden Of Creusa	Kent Von Adeloga	Derby Von Adeloga	Rico Vom Michelstadter Rhthaus
			Ansel Vom Adeloga
		Diwa Vom Loherweg	Vadax Vom Kopenkamp
			Nadja Vom Furstenverg
	Creusa Fair And Fancy From Shepherdwyn	Ch. Tarik Of Ellindale	Ch. Amoulrees Heiko
			Allankee Twopence
		Ice Queen Of Creusa	Sebastionson Of Creusa
			Sheena Of Craggwood

Out-crossing

Out-crossing is the mating of two dogs that are not at all related.

Many breeders use it occasionally after an in-breeding or line-breeding programme so as to introduce new genes and characteristics to the line.

Once the right result has been achieved, line-breeding is then often used to 'fix' this type.

Lornaville Brigadier General: out-cross breeding.

Parents	Grandparents	Great-Grandparents	Great-Great-Grandparents
Ch. Lornaville Mr Bee	Lornaville Ambassador	Ch. Tarquin Of Dawnway	Ch. Eclipse Of Eveley
			Masquerade Of Dawnway
		Balacents Nora Of Lornaville	Ch. Rossfort Oran Of Kenmil
			Almerine Of Balacents
	Lornaville War Lady	Domonic Of Dawnway	Ch. Spartacist Of Hendrawen
			Melody Of Dawnway
		Hargret Rivercroft Brynylon Of Lornaville	Ch. Hendrawen Syrious Norge
			Ch. Harget Rivercroft Nylon
Delridge Kissie	Vornlante Frankie	Ch. Janus Von Insel Wehr	Igor Vom Harberg
			Cessie Vom Konigsbruch
		Willowdale Olga Of Rosetown	Int Ch. Rothick Invictor
			Rosetown Tanya
	Delridge Witty	Piorl Vom Tronje	Lasso Di Val Sole
			Nanni Vom Kirscental
		Delridge Jola	Vegrin Erhard
			Delridge Camilla

CHAPTER EIGHT

HEALTH CARE

Trevor Turner
BVetMed, MRCVS

The German Shepherd Dog is not only large in size (around 60 cms/24 inches to the shoulder) but also in number. Nearly 21,000 were registered with the Kennel Club in 1998 and even more with the American Kennel Club. This, and the fact the breed has been popular both sides of the Atlantic since the 1920s, perhaps explains the reason for the high incidence of problems to which the breed is prone.

Like all working dogs, German Shepherd Dogs are inherently active and have a good brain which needs stimulation. Generally speaking, couch-potato German Shepherds are not contented German Shepherds. However, it has to be accepted that the breed has a number of hereditary and congenital problems.

Breed clubs realise the problems and are doing all in their power to encourage responsible breeding. Epilepsy is one example. A few years ago, the condition was widespread in the breed,

but the problem was recognised and acknowledged and, as a result of careful breeding, epilepsy is no longer a major problem in the breed (although it still occurs sporadically).

Certain conditions in German Shepherd Dogs appear to be associated with an incompetent immune system. This can result in chronic skin or eye conditions. Anal furunculosis (an infection of the skin around the anus), for example, is practically entirely confined to this breed.

PREVENTATIVE CARE

Preventative care involves more than vaccination and parasite control. A correctly balanced diet and regular exercise are also important. Parasite control involves both ectoparasites, e.g. lice, fleas and ticks, and endoparasites, e.g. roundworms, tapeworms and hookworms and also heartworm which is important in southern Europe and the USA.

Vaccination

Vaccination (inoculation) stimulates the dog to produce active immunity against one or a collection of diseases without developing signs of disease. The puppy acquires his first immunity from the dam while in the womb. This is delivered via the bloodstream across the placenta. After birth, the immunity is topped up (boosted) while suckling. This is passive immunity. Once weaned, this immunity soon fades. This is when the puppy should receive its vaccinations. Vaccination is unlikely to last indefinitely and regular boosters are therefore advised.

Inoculation and vaccination are used synonymously throughout the chapter. Strictly, inoculation means introducing the agent to stimulate the immunity into the tissues of the body. It usually involves an injection, but smallpox vaccine, for example, used to be inoculated by scarifying the skin. Vaccination stimulates the subject to produce an immunity against the disease without developing signs. For example, vaccination against infectious tracheitis (kennel cough) using Bordetella vaccine is achieved by instilling a few drops up the nose.

Primary vaccination should be carried out as soon as the passively acquired immunity from the bitch has declined sufficiently to allow the puppy to develop its own immunity to the vaccine. This is usually around 10-12 weeks. Vaccine manufacturers are continuously endeavouring to produce safe, effective vaccines which will ensure ever earlier protection for puppies, so that socialisation can commence as early as possible. This is particularly important in the German Shepherd Dog, where early socialisation can make an immense difference to ultimate temperament, particularly in the case of the shy puppy.

Before the advent of vaccines giving protection at 10-12 weeks, these pups often had to be virtually isolated until approximately four months of age. If inherently shy by nature, introduction to the outside world – when much of their puppyhood had passed – could make integration difficult.

Primary vaccination should occur when the immunity from the mother has run out.

Immunity Gap

The so-called 'immunity gap' has always been a

problem with canine vaccination. In order that the vaccine stimulates the puppy's immunity, circulating maternal antibodies must have fallen sufficiently. The vaccination takes time to stimulate the puppy's active immunity, and, during this period, the puppy is vulnerable to infection. Unfortunately, this happens just at the time when the puppy, particularly a breed such as the German Shepherd Dog, needs to meet as many new experiences as possible in order to mature into a well-integrated family dog.

Once you have acquired your puppy, it is worthwhile ringing your local veterinarian and asking about their vaccination policy. At the same time, you can discuss appointment details, price etc., and whether the practice organises puppy classes or where these are available.

Socialisation classes are extremely useful in the case of the German Shepherd Dog. Although the days of the nervous, neurotic and sometimes nasty German Shepherd are a thing of the past – largely due to the tremendous efforts on the part of concerned breeders – nevertheless, early socialisation with any of the working dogs can do nothing but good; in rapidly growing breeds such as the German Shepherd, the earlier these can be commenced the better.

Boosters

Following primary vaccination, revaccination (boosters) will be necessary at some time or another, although this may not be annually. At the present time, vets on both sides of the Atlantic cannot authoritatively state how often boosters should be administered. Originally, it was advised that boosters should be given annually. This makes economic sense since multivalent vaccines (those containing components against several diseases) cost less overall than vaccination against each individual disease.

Recent concern that some dogs develop adverse reactions to booster vaccination has led to a re-examination of the necessity for annual boosters, particularly since there is evidence that inoculation (vaccination)

Discuss the question of booster vaccinations with your vet.

against certain diseases lasts for much longer than one year.

My personal view is that the risk of reaction is so slight compared with the threat of disease in the unprotected dog that I still tend to go for annual boosters every time. This is based on more than 40 years of clinical experience, during which I encountered distemper, hepatitis and, in the 1980s, parvovirus in epidemic proportions. I have never had to treat a dog with a serious vaccine reaction.

If in doubt, discuss the matter carefully with your vet. The time of the primary vaccination is a good opportunity. Whatever you do, do not omit to have the first protective vaccination course administered, since it is the puppy, once maternal immunity has waned, that is at greatest risk.

' Your vet can advise you on a suitable booster programme '

Can We Measure Immunity?

Blood tests (available both for puppies and adult dogs) will indicate the level of immune response for any of the vaccinated diseases. These give a guide to revaccination. Blood-testing can be expensive, however, since the blood test for each disease will probably cost as much as the combined booster against all the diseases.

Cost apart, is a blood-testing procedure better for the pet? Consider the stress caused to the dog by adopting such a procedure. Taking a blood sample from most puppies and a large proportion of adult German Shepherds is a stressful procedure, considerably more stressful than a booster vaccination which is a simple,

subcutaneous (under the skin) injection, usually done in a flash!

It should be remembered that some vaccines by their very nature do not endow a long-lasting immunity. The intra-nasal **Bordetella bronchiseptica** vaccine against infectious tracheitis (**kennel cough**) only lasts approximately eight months. If you regularly board your dog, or attend training classes, shows, etc., revaccination against infectious tracheitis every six months is money well spent.

Bordetellosis is described as having low mortality and high morbidity; in other words, it does not often prove fatal, but the dog will often cough for several weeks, and, even when apparently recovered, may still be infectious. This is particularly serious if you are attending obedience classes or trying to work your young Shepherd, as it will result in serious disruption of the training programme.

The other components of the cough syndrome are viruses – **adenovirus (hepatitis)**, **distemper virus** and **parainfluenza virus**. These are well covered in the multivalent (multi-disease) vaccines. They usually give a workable immunity for at least a year, maybe longer.

Leptospira vaccines are usually included in the primary vaccination course. These are killed bacterial vaccines and only provide workable immunity in the average dog for about 12 months. Modified live virus vaccines, e.g. distemper, or hepatitis, give a much longer period of protection, but this varies with the individual.

Core vaccines should be given to all puppies.

Due to the efficacy of the multivalent vaccines and the lack of concrete evidence in respect of the adverse effects of boosting, little work has been done to establish exactly how necessary or how often revaccination should be carried out. If you have any anxieties regarding booster vaccinations, take time to discuss the matter with your vet.

Core And Non-core

There is a move in the United States to divide vaccinations into two groups: Core vaccines and Non-core vaccines.

Core vaccines are the necessary ones that protect against a disease that is serious, fatal or difficult to treat. In the UK, this category includes distemper, parvovirus and hepatitis (adenovirus). In the US, rabies is also included.

This is likely to occur in the UK in the not too distant future as a result of the change in quarantine regulations.

Non-core vaccines include Bordetella, Leptospirosis, Coronavirus and Borrelia (Lyme disease) since this latter vaccine is known to cause reactions in a number of dogs.

Canine Distemper

Canine distemper is no longer widespread in the UK, solely due to vaccination. Signs (symptoms) include fever, diarrhoea, coughing and discharges from the nose and eyes. Sometimes the pads harden; this is the so-called hardpad variant. A high proportion of infected dogs develop nervous signs – fits, chorea (twitching of muscle groups) and paralysis. Sometimes the virus is involved in infectious tracheitis.

Hepatitis

Hepatitis (adenovirus disease) has again been successfully combated via vaccination. Signs can vary from sudden death with acute infection to mild cases where the patient is just a bit off-colour. In severe cases, there is usually a fever, enlargement of all the lymph nodes (glands) and a swollen liver. During recovery, the dog can develop 'blue-eye' and may look blind. This is due to oedema (swelling) of the cornea which is the clear part in front of the eye. Although initially worrying, this usually resolves without lasting effects. Adenovirus is also one of the components in infectious tracheitis, or the kennel cough syndrome.

Rabies

Rabies vaccination is mandatory in many countries including the United States, and, with the relaxation of quarantine regulations, may well become so in the UK. It is an extremely serious disease, not only because it is untreatable but also because it is communicable to humans (zoonotic). Modern vaccines are extremely effective in preventing the disease.

Parainfluenza

Multivalent vaccines on both sides of the Atlantic usually include a parainfluenza component. The Bordetella component is not included as it is usually administered as nasal drops. This route of administration gives rapid and effective protection.

Bordetellosis/Infectious Tracheitis

This is not usually life-threatening except in young puppies and old dogs. It causes a persistent cough, and so is also known as 'kennel cough'. In the United Kingdom, the bacterial organism, Bordetella bronchiseptica, is the usual primary cause, although viruses can also be implicated. These include distemper, hepatitis and the parainfluenza virus. In the United States, this latter virus is usually the main cause, with Bordetella as a secondary invader.

Lyme Disease

This is transmitted through tick bites. It is relatively rare in the UK although very common in certain parts of America. It can cause disabling lameness as well as fever and cardiac, kidney and neurological problems.

Kennel cough is highly contagious, and is likely to spread among dogs that live together.

FURTHER PREVENTATIVE CARE

Exercise

Preventative care does not stop with vaccinations. German Shepherds are intelligent working dogs (although now classified in the Pastoral Group in the UK and in the Herding group in the US). They are not sedentary by nature, so a reasonable, regular amount of exercise is essential. With a thick protective coat, battling through icy November rain in a force-10 gale is just as enjoyable and necessary to a healthy and active Shepherd as a quiet walk in the cool of the midsummer evening. We have to accept that exercise is part of the responsibility of owning this active, lively, intelligent dog.

Obesity

Despite all the best efforts at dietary control, some dogs, like some people, inevitably grow fat with age. This affects a small proportion of German Shepherds, just as it does individuals of other breeds.

This small percentage of cases are often not 'people mistakes' – diet has been rigorously controlled, exercise has been regular, but with advancing years the dog has become obese. Problems can soon mount since German Shepherds are perhaps more prone than other breeds to limb problems (including arthritis), and, if overweight, will become reluctant to exercise.

Dogs age just as we do. Unfortunately, they do it quicker, but they still need their regular exercise, albeit suitably modified to take into account age and infirmity. Thus, confronting the icy blasts of winter is a must with the young Shepherd, but could be seriously detrimental to the health of that same dog when arthritic, ten years on.

Parasites

Control of parasites is also part of the preventative health plan that is pivotal to routine care. German Shepherds are working dogs intended for flock duties. Although adaptable and comfortable in a home environment they have an inherent love of the great outdoors and it is not surprising that parasites can be a problem without preventative care. These are **ectoparasites** such as fleas, lice, ticks and mites, or **endoparasites,** of which worms, both roundworms and tapeworms, are the main challenge.

Fleas

Fleas are probably the most common ectoparasites found on dogs and the German Shepherd Dog is no exception. Some carry very high flea burdens without problems, whereas other Shepherds will develop a flea allergy dermatitis, sometimes as the result of only a few

The dog flea – Ctenocephalides canis.

flea bites. The hypersensitivity in these unfortunate dogs is to the flea saliva, causing serious itching. These are the animals that require very vigilant flea control.

Fleas are not host-specific, and both dog and cat fleas can be found on dogs, cats and humans. Hedgehog fleas can also be a problem in German Shepherds kept in urban and suburban gardens in the UK and in northern Europe where hedgehogs are common. In parts of North America, racoons can be the main vector of fleas. Human fleas are very rare, but all types can bite people and other animals.

The eggs and larval forms of the flea develop off the host. Development time depends upon humidity and temperature. In warm environments, the life-cycle is completed in days rather than weeks. This is one of the reasons why fleas are such a problem in the UK in summertime and in the southern states of North America all the year round.

Effective flea control involves both adult fleas on the dog and the immature stages which develop in the environment. Obviously, control of developing fleas in the garden (yard) is not practicable, particularly if the area is continuously re-infested from visiting hedgehogs or racoons. Fleas have to have a meal of blood to complete their life-cycle. They feed on the dog, then lay eggs which develop in the environment. Development of the next generation, depending on the temperature and humidity, can be as short as three weeks.

Fleas can also survive in suitable environments for more than a year without feeding. This is the reason why dogs – and people – can get

Oral medication to prevent fleas may be more effective than using a spray in long-coated dogs.

bitten when entering properties left unoccupied for quite long periods.

Flea Control

Preventative methods in the home should include thorough vacuuming to remove immature stages. The use of an environmental insecticide with prolonged action to kill any developing fleas must also be considered since few insecticides currently on the market will kill flea larvae.

Treatment of your dog can be with oral medication, which prevents completion of the life-cycle of the flea, as well as the use of sprays, powders or spot-on preparations to kill any adult fleas present. Insecticidal baths effectively kill adult fleas in the coat but do not have any residual effect. Therefore bathing must be combined with other methods of flea control.

' Insecticides can be lethal if used or abused '

Probably more effective than sprays or powders are modern spot-on preparations which will give reasonable protection lasting up to two months, even if your dog is bathed between applications. They disperse the chemical without it getting into the body, spreading it through the fat layer beneath the skin. Very quickly – within 24 hours – the dog will have total protection against fleas. When a flea bites the dog, it penetrates through the fat layer to get to the blood, and thus ingests the chemical.

If your German Shepherd has a flea allergy dermatitis, you must use something to kill the adult fleas and so prevent your dog being bitten and injected with flea saliva, which causes the itching. Oral medication preventing completion

of the life-cycle is very effective for long-term control, but does nothing to the mature fleas which are biting the hypersensitive pet for that all-essential blood meal.

Before using any treatment, you must read the manufacturer's instructions carefully. If in any doubt about the suitability of a product for your pet, seek veterinary advice.

Lice

Lice are not as common as fleas and usually require direct contact for transmission. The whole of the life-cycle occurs on the host and the eggs (nits) are attached to individual hairs. In the UK, they are not uncommonly seen on puppies bred in winter time in rural locations.

Infestation is usually associated with violent scratching, and the lice and nits can usually be seen, particularly on the ears and around the head and elbows. Bathing in insecticidal shampoos suitable for fleas is effective.

Ticks

Ticks can be a problem in some areas. In suburbia, they are frequently carried on hedgehogs; in rural areas, sheep are usually the primary host.

In America certain ticks can be carriers of Lyme disease.

As with fleas and lice, there are a variety of insecticidal products available; some of the spot-on preparations have prolonged activity even if the dog is bathed between applications.

Harvest Mites

These are tiny red larvae of a mite that lives freely (i.e. it is not parasitic). The adult lives in decaying organic matter. The mite is particularly prevalent in areas with a chalky soil and the bright orange to red larval mites are just visible to the naked eye.

The German Shepherd Dog exercised in fields and damp woodland locations can be particularly prone to catching them. They cause intense irritation and dermatitis. The continuous licking can often result in dark stains affecting all the feet. The dermatitis can also occur on the muzzle and parts of the head.

The use of prolonged-action insecticidal sprays is recommended since reinfestation is likely.

Mange

Perhaps because some German Shepherd Dogs are less than adequately immuno-competent, mange can be a problem in the breed. It is a parasitic skin disease caused by microscopic mites, two of which are important in the dog.

One, the **Demodectic mite**, lives in the hair follicles, and as long as the dog's immune system is functioning, these mites cause no harm. However, if there is an immune system problem, the demodectic mites can cause hair loss in patches, particularly on the face and around the eyes.

Compared with Scabies or Sarcoptic mange, the other common form of mange, demodectic mange does not appear to be particularly itchy.

' Two types of mange can affect the GSD '

Also, since it manifests itself in the immuno-incompetent dog, it is not particularly contagious. There are very effective remedies available, but treatment has to be under veterinary supervision.

By contrast, **Sarcoptic mange** is very itchy. In the UK and parts of Europe, the main source of infection is the fox. Unlike Demodectic mange, Sarcoptic mange is also highly contagious to other dogs and also to humans, particularly children.

Diagnosis with both types of mange depends on identification of the causal mite under a microscope. Various dips and shampoos are available for treatment, but, again, veterinary advice is necessary.

Endoparasites

Although worms are by far the most important endoparasites as far as your dog is concerned, do remember there are others. Coccidia and Giardia, which are tiny, one-celled organisms, can occasionally cause chronic diarrhoea and lack of growth in German Shepherd Dog puppies. However, roundworms and tapeworms are by far the most common endoparasities.

Roundworms

Nematodes, or roundworms, are the most common worms in the dog. Because of their complicated life-cycle and the fact that puppies can be born with worms acquired from their mother before birth, roundworms are virtually ubiquitous in puppies.

The most common roundworm is *Toxocara canis*. It is a large, round, white worm 7-15 cms (3-6 inches) long. There are many effective worm treatments, but few are effective against the larval (juvenile) stages. Roundworm larvae remain dormant in the tissue of adult dogs but in the bitch, under the influence of the hormones of pregnancy, they become activated, cross the placenta and enter the puppy, where they finally develop into adult worms in the small intestine. The larvae are also passed from bitch to puppy in the milk, and also via the faeces.

There is a slight risk that humans can become infected with roundworms from dogs, so adult dogs should be wormed routinely about twice a year. Larvae develop rapidly in a puppy's body, so your pup should be wormed from approximately two weeks of age, and treatment should be repeated regularly until the puppy is at least six months old. Discuss an effective worming strategy with your vet.

In the puppy, a heavy infestation causes many problems, from generalised ill-health to diarrhoea and vomiting, obstruction of the bowel and even death. Adult dogs can carry heavy worm burdens if not regularly wormed and show surprisingly few symptoms.

Tapeworms

Tapeworms, or cestodes, are the other major class of worms found in the dog. Unlike roundworms, they have an indirect life-cycle so spread is not directly from dog to dog. Intermediate hosts vary from fleas to horses, depending on the type of tapeworm.

The most common tapeworm in the dog is **Dipylidium caninum** for which fleas are the intermediate host. Flea larvae swallow the microscopic tapeworm eggs shed by the dog in the faeces. These mature as the flea develops. The dog consumes the flea and so the life-cycle is completed.

Dipylidium is a large worm and can measure up to 50 cm (20 inches). Individual segments which are passed in the faeces resemble small rice grains around the dog's anus. These mature segments are all packed with eggs which have to be eaten by the intermediate host to complete the life-cycle.

Effective remedies are available without prescription but it is important that fleas are also controlled, so it is worth discussing this with your vet.

Other species of tapeworm have intermediate hosts that include sheep, horses and rodents. There is little danger to the dog provided raw flesh of the infested intermediate host is not fed or scavenged (e.g. a rabbit carcass).

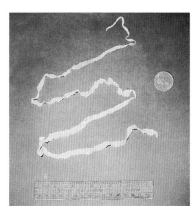

Tapeworm passed by an adult dog. (The coin gives an indication of size.)

Other Worms

Hookworms and **Whipworms** are other types of worms that can affect the bowel. These are generally only a problem in kennel dogs that have grass runs. Modern multi-wormers will eradicate.

Canine lungworm (*Filaroides oslerei*) can be a problem in Shepherd puppies and young dogs. The worms live in nodules in the air passages and cause coughing and loss of condition. Veterinary treatment is available.

The responsible owner should be able to follow basic first aid procedures.

Heartworm caused by the roundworm *Dirofilaria immitis* is a major problem in many warmer parts of the world. It can occur in Great Britain in imported animals. Transmission is by bites from mosquitoes and very effective remedies are available.

EMERGENCY CARE AND FIRST AID

First aid is the initial treatment given in an emergency immediately after injury, collapse or sudden onset of illness. The purpose is to preserve life, reduce pain and discomfort and minimise the risk of permanent disability or disfigurement. First aid is essential if your Shepherd is convulsing and/or is unconscious (collapsed), has breathing problems, is bleeding and/or is in shock.

Irrespective of the emergency, there is much that can be done by simple first aid.

1. Keep calm and do not panic.
2. Wherever possible get help. Contact your veterinary surgeon, explain the situation and obtain first aid advice.
3. If there is a possible injury, keep your pet as still as possible. With the German Shepherd this often involves placing the dog on his side with the head and neck gently pressed to the ground, with your arm across the neck, if necessary holding the uninjured limbs.
4. If shocked, keep him warm by putting a blanket or some clothing over him.

5. If there is a possibility of broken bones, particularly if the spine is involved, try to keep the dog as still as possible.

6. Take your Shepherd to the vet as soon as possible. If he cannot walk, try lifting him on a blanket carried between at least two people. If the injuries involve the back end, you may be able to move him by grasping him firmly around the chest and letting the hindquarters hang. In this way you are unlikely to cause further injuries.

7. If you do not have an estate car, place him on a blanket on the back seat and ensure someone travels in the back with him.

8. Drive carefully and observe the speed limits.

Shock

Shock is a complex condition which results in a serious fall in blood pressure. Causes include blood loss due to bleeding, heart failure, acute allergy and heat stroke.

First signs include rapid breathing and increased heart rate. The mucous membranes of the gums, lips and under the eyelids look very pale, the dog may be depressed, and may vomit, and his feet or ears may feel cold.

Warmth is important. Cover with coats, blankets or even newspaper. Keep him quiet and seek immediate veterinary help, particularly if there is bleeding (which should be controlled if possible).

Airway

Try to keep the airway clear to allow oxygen to the lungs. If your Shepherd has swallowed a

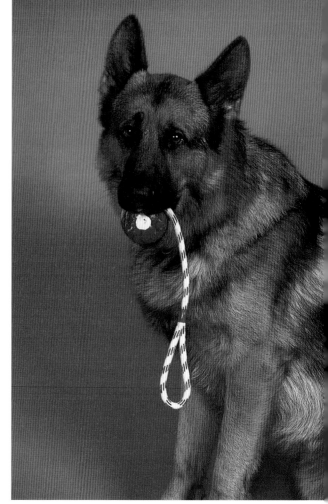

Always ensure balls and toys are too large to be swallowed.

ball, has vomited or collapsed, or is choking, it is important that you do your best to ensure that the airway is unobstructed.

Do not put your fingers in the mouth. The dog will be just as frightened as you are, and, if fighting for his life, may well bite with panic.

Using a tie or a pair of tights, it is sometimes possible to loop material around the upper and lower fang teeth and to open the mouth. If there is an obstruction that can be removed, attempt it. Sometimes balls get stuck in the throat and can be expelled by pressing quite forcibly behind the lower jaw bones (mandibles). This is not an uncommon emergency seen in the Shepherd. Make sure that adult dogs do not play with balls the size of tennis balls or smaller!

If your dog is not breathing, try gently pumping the chest with your hand, just behind the elbows. Also at the same site, see if you can feel a heartbeat. If not, try cardiac massage. With a hand on each side of the rib cage, just behind the elbows which are pulled slightly forward, gently squeeze the ribs over the heart.

Bleeding

Torn nails are not uncommon. They are extremely painful and bleed profusely, as do cut pads. A tight bandage can be improvised from any reasonably clean material. If bandaging material isn't available, a plastic bag secured snugly over the paw can be used to quell the haemorrhage.

If a tight bandage has been applied, do not leave it on for more than 15-20 minutes. If the site cannot be bandaged, endeavour to stem serious haemorrhage by applying finger or hand pressure, and try to get help to transport your dog to the vet immediately.

Burns And Scalds

Cool the burned area with cold water as quickly as possible. Cover with damp towels. If the burn is due to a caustic substance, try to dilute this using plenty of cold water.

If your dog has licked caustic (e.g. drain-cleaner, bleach etc.) try washing out the mouth using cloths soaked in clean, cold water, pressed between the jaws.

Heat Stroke

Heat stroke occurs rapidly and is frequently the result of dogs being left in cars in sultry weather. *Remember that the car need not necessarily be in direct sunlight to kill your dog.*

First signs are excessive panting with obvious distress. Unconsciousness and coma quickly follow. Try to reduce body temperature by bathing in copious amounts of cold water, then cover the still wet animal in damp towels and

Heat stroke occurs very rapidly when a dog is left in a car with insufficient ventilation.

take him to the vet as soon as possible. If he is not able to walk, carry him on a blanket.

Eye Injuries

These are usually the result of trauma (e.g. cats' claws, bushes etc.). Cover the eye with a pad soaked in cold water, or, better still, saline solution (contact lens solution). Veterinary help should be sought.

Fits And Seizures

Some German Shepherd Dogs can be prone to epileptic fits. Do not touch the dog, as he should not be stimulated while in the seizure. Left alone, he is unlikely to injure himself, particularly if any movable furniture, (stools etc.) are moved out of his way. Try to darken the area (draw the curtains), as this speeds recovery.

Once recovered, he will be dazed and unable to see or hear properly for a short time. Take care handling him because he may be frightened and not recognise you. As soon as practicable, take him to your vet.

If the fit lasts more than three or four minutes, contact your veterinary surgeon for advice.

BREED-SPECIFIC CONDITIONS

With their huge popularity stretching back over more than five decades, German Shepherds do seem to have attracted certain breed-prone conditions. As already mentioned, some of these problems may be due to faults in the immune system. The diseases which follow are not intended in any way to be a comprehensive list, but do give some indication of the more common problems found in the breed.

Anal Furunculosis

Anal furunculosis is like a carbuncle or a many-headed abscess in the anal region. In the UK and the US, it is a disease that affects the German Shepherd Dog more than any other breed. Often the condition is only detected during a routine veterinary examination.

Causes are not fully understood, although impaction of the anal glands and poor ventilation due to the close-lying tail have been suggested. The condition may have an auto-immune basis and a genetic predisposition.

In mild cases, medical treatment is often effective. Therefore always check your Shepherd's bottom during grooming sessions. If at all worried, consult your veterinary surgeon.

Anal Glands

Dogs and bitches of all breeds have two small scent glands either side of the anus. This is one of the reasons why dogs, when greeting each other, sniff each other's backsides. The conformation of the Shepherd, with the close-lying tail over the anus, is considered to be one of the reasons why these glands can cause problems, often resulting in anal abscesses or furunculosis (see above).

Symptoms of anal gland problems are excessive licking of the anal region and often an unpleasant odour. If worried, consult your vet.

Allergic Skin Disease

Allergic skin diseases are among the most common, difficult and frustrating problems to diagnose and treat in veterinary medicine. Allergic (hypersensitivity) reactions occur when the dog's immune system overreacts to a foreign substance. This leads to tissue damage and, commonly, intense itching. The most common foreign substance is flea saliva, causing flea allergy dermatitis, but sometimes food constituents, inhaled particles (usually pollens) and contact allergies can be involved. The result is a very unhappy dog with very itchy skin.

' Food allergies are common in the German Shepherd '

Food allergies are also common in the German Shepherd. These cause not only skin problems but bowel problems too. A food allergy can develop after the dog has been fed the same diet for many years. Consult your vet, who may refer you to a veterinary dermatologist.

Atopy is an inhalant allergy. In the German Shepherd, it is often due to certain pollens (e.g. grass) acting as the allergen. Affected individuals are itchy and may rub and scratch their faces, particularly around the eyes and ears. They may also chew their feet. Veterinary dermatologists can carry out tests to determine the specific allergen causing the condition.

Cardiac Problems

There are a number of heart conditions that can affect the German Shepherd.

• **Patent ductus arteriosus (PDA)**
In the foetus, the ductus arteriosus is a direct connection between the main pulmonary artery and the aorta so that the majority of the circulating blood bypasses the non-functional lungs. At birth, this vessel should close in order that the puppy oxygenates its blood via its now functional lungs. Failure of the duct to close results in blood being pumped back to the lungs (causing overload) and not to the rest of the body where it is needed. This results in stunted growth.

The puppy appears to fatigue easily and does not grow. There is often difficulty in breathing and a cough is present. Surgery is successful if the condition is diagnosed early enough.

• **Vascular ring anomaly (or persistent right aortic arch)**
Due to a congenital abnormality, certain blood vessels formed during the development of the foetus do not disappear as they should and at birth the oesophagus (gullet) is trapped within an encircling ring of these vessels. As the puppy grows, this ring causes difficulty in swallowing; at weaning, frequent regurgitation of food will be noted.

Since food cannot pass through the constriction easily, this leads to an enlargement of the oesophagus (megaoesophagus) as the food accumulates. Surgery can be successful provided an early diagnosis is made.

• **Chronic degenerative radiculomyelopathy (CDRM)** is not uncommon in the older German Shepherd. Affected dogs show a slowly progressive loss of use of the hindlegs. An early sign is knuckling of the hind paws, especially when the dog is turning a corner. Ultimately, bowel control can be lost. The condition is non-painful, although the lameness is distressing for owners. The cause is unknown but may be immune-mediated, the body attempting to destroy its own nervous tissue. Treatment is often unrewarding. Since the condition is non-painful, some owners find that paralysis carts help to prevent drag injuries.

Eye Problems

Pannus, or **chronic superficial keratitis (CSK)** is non-painful, but can interfere with vision, and it is progressive. Drugs can very successfully control the problem. Again, the problem may be immune-mediated in origin.

Bone Disorder

Hip and **elbow dysplasia** are common conditions in German Shepherds. The joint British Veterinary Association/Kennel Club eradication scheme in the UK (with similar schemes in other countries), is doing much to improve the situation.

Dysplasia means abnormal growth. Hips are most commonly affected, but elbows and other joints can also be implicated. It is a multifactorial disease, with heredity, nutrition, trauma, and exercise all influencing the outcome of the condition. When purchasing a pedigree German Shepherd Dog puppy, ask if the parents have been X-rayed.

For affected dogs, all is not lost. Modern drugs and, if need be, surgery, can at least ensure that a significant number of affected dogs can enjoy a normal, active life.

Overexercising youngsters can cause permanent damage to vulnerable joints.

Ununited anconeal process is another developmental anomaly seen predominantly in the German Shepherd Dog. It can coexist with other forms of joint abnormality. Signs are progressive unilateral or bilateral forelimb lameness which usually starts at about four or five months of age. Examination of the elbow joint will indicate pain with reduced joint movement. Left untreated, the joint instability leads to a condition called DJD (degenerative joint disease) which is a chronic progressive arthritis. If you think your young Shepherd shows any lameness, consult your veterinarian without delay. Modern treatments are available that can restore normal mobility.

Epilepsy, Seizures Or Fits

These can sometimes be due to liver, renal or cardiac problems. Sometimes fits occur with no apparent abnormalities, and blood tests are normal. This is idiopathic epilepsy and can be hereditary in the German Shepherd. Modern drug therapy will control the condition so that the majority of patients can lead perfectly normal lives.

Some epileptic Shepherds excel as working dogs, even entering Obedience competitions and working trials. Treatment is a long-term commitment, although some dogs can gradually be weaned from their anticonvulsants. If you have a German Shepherd Dog that has one fit, this does not mean that he has epilepsy, but if the fits are recurrent, epilepsy has to be considered. When considering a puppy, ask about epilepsy in the line.

DIGESTIVE PROBLEMS

Diarrhoea

Dogs normally pass formed faeces which retain their shape, between one to three times a day.

Diarrhoea is the frequent passage of faeces that are unformed and can actually be liquid and are increased in volume. Diarrhoea is common in many dogs and particularly so in the German Shepherd. **Acute diarrhoea** is rapid in onset and may be due to simple overeating or scavenging decomposed remains, etc. Infectious causes – bacteria, viruses or protozoal organisms – may be involved, as can irritant poisons, sometimes dietary allergies. In the simple case, withholding food for 24 hours but offering small quantities of liquids (usually water) at frequent intervals is often all that is necessary to bring about improvement.

If diarrhoea persists, or is recurrent, it is termed **chronic diarrhoea** and it is to this that the German Shepherd appears particularly prone. Although causes as above can be implicated, there are others. Food intolerances (allergies), digestive abnormalities and immune-mediated problems may be implicated.

Offer small quantities of water if you are withholding food for a limited period.

Some food intolerances may be obvious at weaning: for example, some puppies may not be able to digest cow's milk, often due to the increased lactose or milk sugar compared with bitch's milk which can cause diarrhoea.

Other intolerances may be due to allergic reactions to particular types of food. For example, some dogs may become allergic to beef protein, the feeding of which will cause diarrhoea. Treatment requires veterinary help and complicated trial elimination of suspected foods, and ultimately diet modification.

Exocrine pancreatic insufficiency (EPI) is a common digestive problem in the German Shepherd. This results in insufficient production or complete absence of essential digestive enzymes which enter the bowel by the pancreatic duct and are involved in the digestion of fats, carbohydrates and proteins. EPI in the German Shepherd can be congenital (present from birth) or acquired, often due to injury or infection, and the signs are usually a voraciously hungry dog that never puts on weight, and passes copious quantities of fatty, loose or semi-formed faeces. Accurate treatment and diagnosis is available but treatment usually involves control rather than cure and can be a lifetime commitment, both in terms of cost and attention to diet.

Another common condition causing chronic diarrhoea is so-called **bacterial overgrowth** which, in simple terms, can be thought of as an excessive growth of certain bowel bacteria which affects the digestion and absorption of food, and so results in chronic diarrhoea. This is thought to be part of a lack of proper immune control in some cases and can be treated with antibiotics, but often these have to be administered long-term.

In the case of **allergic diarrhoea** the allergens (often foods) may also cause allergic skin problems, usually resulting in itching, hair loss etc.

Dysentery

If the diarrhoea is particularly watery and contains blood, this is dysentery. Contact with your vet is essential. Causes can vary from injury to the bowel as a result of eating foreign objects to viruses (e.g. parvovirus) and some allergies.

Gastritis (Inflammation Of The Stomach)

Gastritis, especially acute (short-lived) gastritis, is common in all dogs. It can often be due to eating contaminated or decomposing food, trash, bones, grass or foreign bodies (such as pebbles or pieces of metal). It can also sometimes occur in very nervous German Shepherds and can be associated with gastric ulcers.

' The first rule in first aid is not to panic '

Initially, acute gastritis should be treated by withholding food for 24 hours and offering only small quantities of fluid at frequent intervals. If vomiting continues, veterinary help is necessary, since further investigation may be warranted.

Gastric Dilation/Torsion

This condition, also known as GDV (gastric dilation and volvulus), is always an acute emergency. If your dog appears 'blown up' or at all uncomfortable, especially after a meal, consult your vet without delay.

The rapid enlargement of the stomach (dilation) may be due to overeating, especially in young dogs, and can be self-cured by vomiting. In older animals, the cause is not so clear. Gas accumulation may be due to eating too quickly or due to fermentation of food actually in the stomach.

The abdomen rapidly distends and in large, deep-chested dogs such as the German Shepherd, the blown-up stomach may rotate upon itself within the abdomen causing extreme discomfort, as well as interfering with the blood supply. This results in the onset of acute shock and gangrene of the devitalised stomach wall.

Dogs prone to gas (flatus) after eating should be fed smaller meals more frequently, but if in doubt, veterinary advice should always be sought, since an alteration in diet may be advised.

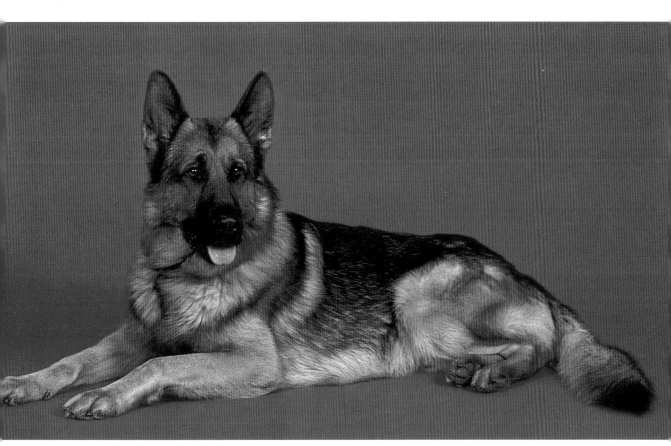

The observant owner will know their dog well, and so will be able to spot any sign of trouble at an early stage.

Megaoesophagus

Mentioned above in connection with vascular ring anomaly (persistent right aortic arch), megaoesophagus can also occur in the breed due to other causes, for example a defect in the nerve supply preventing it from contracting properly, or injury following the swallowing of foreign bodies or corrosives. Food does not pass into the stomach and accumulates in the gullet or oesophagus which gradually enlarges. The condition can occur in puppies and adult dogs, and results in regurgitation of food soon after eating.

Food usually comes to rest in that portion of the oesophagus which passes horizontally through the chest above the heart; as the wall of the oesophagus stretches, so the food is held longer before it is returned.

Some forms of megaoesophagus, particularly in puppies, are curable, but, in the adult dog, tremendous commitment is necessary.

Von Willebrand's Disease

This is an hereditary defect of blood platelets which causes prolonged bleeding (due to lack of clotting) in some German Shepherds. The condition can be tested for with a simple blood test which determines the amount of von Willebrand factor (vWF) in the sample. This gives a direct indication of the clotting capacity of the blood. This test is well worthwhile, particularly if your dog has to undergo any major surgery.

This list of breed-prone problems is not intended to be exhaustive; nevertheless, it is lengthy compared with some other breeds.

Despite their potential health problems, these loyal, intelligent, wonderful-looking animals largely live to a ripe old age and give an incredible amount of pleasure in return for your care and understanding.